Gambon:
a Life in Acting

Mel Gussow has contributed four other volumes to a parallel series, *Conversations with Pinter, Conversations with Stoppard, Conversations with (and about) Beckett* and *Conversations with Miller*. He is also the author of the biography, *Edward Albee: A Singular Journey*, and is the co-editor of the Library of America's two-volume edition of the plays of Tennessee Williams.

As a longtime drama critic for the *New York Times*, he was the winner of the George Jean Nathan Award for Dramatic Criticism, and is currently a cultural writer for the same paper.

His other books include *Theatre on the Edge: New Visions, New Voices*, a collection of theatre reviews and essays, and *Don't Say Yes Until I Finish Talking*, a biography of Darryl F. Zanuck. He has written profiles for the *New Yorker* and other magazines. He lives in New York City and is a frequent visitor to London as an observer of the British theatrical scene.

Mel Gussow

Gambon:
a Life in Acting

Nick Hern Books
London
www.nickhernbooks.co.uk

for Ann

A Nick Hern Book

Gambon: a Life in Acting first published in Great Britain in 2004 by Nick Hern Books Ltd, 14 Larden Road, London W3 7ST

Copyright © 2004 Mel Gussow

Mel Gussow has asserted his right to be identified as the author of this work

Typeset by Country Setting, Kingsdown, Kent CT14 8ES
Printed and bound in Great Britain by Biddles, King's Lynn

A CIP catalogue record for this book is available from the British Library

ISBN 1 85459 773 6 (hardback)
ISBN 1 85459 806 6 (paperback)

Contents

Introduction

During his years as head of Britain's National Theatre, Peter Hall always wanted to present a revival of Brecht's *The Life of Galileo*. Finally, when he had obtained the rights to the play from the Brecht estate and had the financing for the production, he turned to the question of casting. Colin Blakely and Albert Finney were high on the list of logical candidates for the monumental role, but Hall – to the astonishment of his associates – reached down into the ranks of those who had worked at the National and chose Michael Gambon, who had built his reputation principally in plays by Alan Ayckbourn, Simon Gray and Harold Pinter. At the time, Gambon was appearing, under Hall's direction, in Pinter's *Betrayal*. Although Gambon was admired as an actor, he was not generally considered to have the weight or the authority for Galileo. Hall felt differently. He believed that Gambon was 'a gentle actor' but also one with 'catastrophic power'. Others were unconvinced, and several directors rejected the project precisely because of their doubts about the actor's suitability.

Eventually, John Dexter agreed to direct the play and when *Galileo* opened it became a transforming experience for the actor. Gambon not only rose to the challenge but far exceeded all expectations. He was, in fact, a masterly Galileo, rivalling memories of Charles Laughton, who had created the part for Brecht, setting a standard for those who might be daring enough to follow him.

On opening night, 13 August 1980, with bravos echoing through the Olivier Theatre, Gambon returned to his dressing room on a wave of euphoria. At the National, the dressing rooms are aligned on four levels surrounding a quadrangle.

As he started to remove his make-up, he heard applause from across the quadrangle and walked to the window to investigate. The applause grew to a roar of approval. All the actors – and there were more than forty in the company – came to their windows and gave him a long and thunderous ovation. This spontaneous collective tribute to a fellow actor from a normally restrained and competitive group of people was unprecedented in the history of the National. 'I stood at the window and wept my eyes out,' Gambon recalled. The next day, the critics followed with their accolades in print. A major classical actor had been discovered.

Ayckbourn was one of many people who were elated by Gambon's triumph. He said that when Gambon appeared in his comedies he had been 'using about a fifteenth of his range,' and added, 'We were using a sledgehammer to crack nuts with.' The play unlocked career doors for Gambon. 'It tipped me into the heavyweight league,' he said. In the years that followed, he has moved back and forth, with equal brilliance, from classics (Shakespeare) to contemporary plays (Samuel Beckett, Harold Pinter, David Hare, Caryl Churchill), from tragedy to comedy, and was soon recognised as the most protean and prodigious of English actors.

Before *Galileo*, Sir Ralph Richardson began calling him 'The Great Gambon'. That was, Gambon said, as if Richardson considered him 'a circus act'. In a metaphorical sense, it is not an inaccurate characterisation. As an actor, Gambon is both a high-wire trapeze flier and a clown doing pratfalls in the sawdust: after galvanizing audiences in *Galileo*, he conquered King Lear and then Antony in *Antony and Cleopatra* at Stratford-upon-Avon. As Lear, he could also play the fool, toying with Cordelia's suitors as he referred with almost incestuous envy to their 'amorous sojourns'. But he never sacrificed Lear's stature, and even as he succumbed to madness he had moments of blinding sanity. Performed in repertory, *King Lear* and *Antony and Cleopatra* were a double tour de force for Gambon, especially on those days when *Lear* was done at the matinee and *Antony* followed in the evening. After playing an 80-year-old Lear, Gambon said, it was 'like a holiday' to play a 40-year-old Antony, opposite Helen Mirren.

At the same time, he is also a farceur of uncommon distinction. He has caused theatregoers literally to fall into the aisles with rollicking laughter. In an actor's equivalent of the trapeze artist's triple somersault in mid-air, he played three totally disparate roles in the 1986-87 season at the National. He was a buffoon of a butler in a revival of the old Aldwych farce *Tons of Money*. Standing at a perpetual tilt, leaning against a door or against another actor – as each is about to give way – he was like a good-natured Quasimodo. In Ayckbourn's serious comedy, *A Small Family Business*, he was a seemingly incorruptible entrepreneur turned gangster. Most challenging of all, he offered a visceral incarnation of Eddie Carbone, the Italian-American longshoreman in Arthur Miller's *A View from the Bridge*. From the moment he walked on stage, with a movement that was both graceful and lumbering, he was Eddie Carbone on the hoof, a man who, in Gambon's interpretation, was almost too large for his body.

For Americans who were not frequent travellers to London, Gambon was unknown until *The Singing Detective*, Dennis Potter's 1986 fantasy-filled film noir for television, in which the actor gave a mesmerising performance as an imaginative invalid with delusions of private-eye grandeur. I had seen him act for the first time in London in the summer of 1976. I went to see Simon Gray's *Otherwise Engaged*, and was disappointed to learn that the star, Alan Bates, had left the cast and had been replaced by Gambon. As it turned out, he was splendid in the central role of the coolly unemotional publisher. I began following his career, but had no idea that in scarcely more than 10 years, he would rise to the very peak of his profession. By 1987, I would write an essay in the *New York Times* headlined, 'A Virtuoso Who Specializes in Everything,' which would say: 'Role for role, pound for pound, Michael Gambon is, arguably, the finest actor in the English theatre.'

Harold Pinter has worked with Gambon in diverse capacities – as a playwright, a director, a screenwriter and even as a fellow actor (in a radio version of *Betrayal*). 'There is no question about it,' he said in 1990, 'over the past 14 years a great actor has come about. He really has just about everything – enormous power, great depth, absolute expertise. He goes for the heart of the matter, and does it most economically and totally without sentimentality. He can arrest and compel. At the centre of all this, he is a most delicate actor. I've worked with Olivier, Richardson, Gielgud, Scofield, Redgrave, Guinness and Peggy Ashcroft, the greats of English acting, and Michael Gambon is in that category.' In 2003, Deborah Warner, who directed him in the film *Last September* (but not yet on stage), said, 'I think he is one of the greatest actors there ever, ever was. I think he is the thing itself, the real acting creature.'

Olivier represented passion, Gielgud lyricism and Ralph Richardson, the most underrated of the three, was the supreme character actor. No-one would ever confuse Gambon with Gielgud – Ian McKellen would be a closer comparison – but he combines the boldness of Olivier with the blissful eccentricity of Richardson. Yet Gambon is an absolute original. Ayckbourn, who directed him in all three plays at the National in the 1986-87 season, said, 'Working with him is like having some wonderful, limitless machine, like a Lamborghini, at your disposal as director and writer.' That was a precise image, especially considering Gambon's own non-academic background in industry. An unprepossessing working-class man, he left school at 15, signed on as an apprentice engineer and later entered the theatre without any formal training as an actor. Somehow, through talent, determination, and – he would say – luck, he arrived at his position of eminence.

Gambon learned on the job, at first in amateur theatre, and, at 23, as a member – a very lowly member – of Olivier's original National Theatre company at the Old Vic (from 1963 to 1967). In those early days at the National, Gambon played the smallest of roles, but took advantage of being part of the company. With his mates, he studied Olivier closely, trying to understand what made him a great actor. Reaching for guidelines, they found symbols. Noticing that Olivier habitually wore a copper band around his wrist, ostensibly to ward off rheumatism, the younger actors began wearing identical copper bands. To this day, Gambon wears a huge, blockish ring on his little finger, like those worn by Gielgud and Paul Scofield. Amulets and heirlooms can enrich an actor's feeling of consanguinity – the sense that what he does occurs in a grand context.

Increasingly, actors train for the theatre as they might train for professions like law or medicine. Annually, young men and women march out of Oxford and Cambridge, the Royal Academy of Dramatic Art (RADA) and London's Central School of Speech and Drama and make their mark in the theatre. Often they go to work in companies run by other graduates of Oxford and Cambridge

Gambon's Cambridge was the Vickers Armstrong factory in Kent, and his RADA was amateur theatre in North London. He had less than a high-school education and no knowledge of theatre as either literature or performance. When he first appeared in classics, he had neither read nor seen the plays in which he was performing. That remained true even as he graduated to larger roles. There are still enormous gaps in his background. He does not often read plays, including Shakespeare, except when he is offered a role in one. In a field that encourages feelings of self-importance and narcissism, he is resolutely down-to-earth. It might be said that Gambon is a rude mechanical, like Bottom the weaver or Snug the joiner, but one who became a great actor.

Michael John Gambon was born in Dublin on 19 October 1940, the first of three children in the family of Edward and Mary Gambon. Nowhere in the family tree is there anyone remotely resembling an artist. The Gambons were definably working class. At the beginning of the Second World War, Edward Gambon moved to London to look for work. During the war, he was a reserve policeman. In 1945, his family joined him in London, and he took a job in a factory. The

11

Gambons settled in Camden Town, in North London. There was never a thought of Michael having a higher education, and, in any case, his grades would probably not have allowed him to attend a university. In 1955, living with his parents near Crayford in North Kent, he left school and took a job sweeping floors and serving tea in a factory that made radio and television sets. Soon he moved to a nearby tool-and-die works, to which he was attracted because the employees wore white coats. Then, after passing a qualifying examination, he shifted to Vickers Armstrong, which made everything from shotguns to sewing machines; he signed indentures to begin a five-year apprenticeship leading to a job as a tool-and-die maker. By then, he was 16 – and he loved the work.

One day, he walked past the Erith Playhouse, an amateur theatre near his home, and noticed a sign that read 'Backstage Help Required.' He was drawn through the door, and volunteered to work as a set builder, without pay. Because of his mechanical aptitude, the work came easily. He had never gone to a play, although he thought that the theatre might be vaguely related to the James Dean movies he saw at his local cinema. He drifted from carpentry into acting. His first bit part was in a forgotten one-act play called *Orange Blossom.* To his astonishment, he liked being onstage. 'I went *varoom!*' he recalls. 'I thought, Jesus, this is for me. I want to be an actor.' In theatre, he also found a sense of family.

In 1957, looking for theatrical work, he came across an advertisement in a theatre magazine. The ad, placed by the long-established, left-wing Unity Theatre in North London, read, 'Actors and actresses always required for near-professional productions.' He remembered that when he was six years old he had played in the street outside the Unity. After joining the company, Gambon once again moved from set construction to acting. Throughout his teens, he worked a double shift – in the factory in Kent by day and in amateur theatricals in London by night. The factory workers who knew about his moonlighting scoffed. They thought acting was sissy.

He began to think that theatre might become at least a near-profession, and in 1962 sent a number of letters applying for employment. One of the applications went to Hilton Edwards and Micheál MacLiammóir, the celebrated actor-managers of the Gate Theatre in Dublin. Gambon invented a résumé, moving his amateur roles into the professional category and making up others. After Edwards agreed to a meeting, Gambon flew to Dublin. Asked what roles he had played recently, he quickly answered, Marchbanks in *Candida* in the West End. Apologising for not being able to offer him any good parts, Edwards asked him if he would play the Second Gentleman of Cyprus in *Othello*. This struck Gambon as an insignificant offer to someone who had just played Marchbanks in the West End, but, having never played Marchbanks and having never been near the West End, he did not hesitate to accept the offer.

Following the Dublin engagement and a brief European tour with the Irish company, the Second Gentleman of Cyprus returned to London and began actively pursuing his new career while keeping half a hand in his old one. He was an understudy in Spike Milligan's absurdist comedy, *The Bed-sitting Room* at the Duke of York's Theatre. When the actor whom Gambon understudied wanted to take a night off, he paid Gambon a pound to go on in his place. In January of 1963, at the age of 22, Gambon faced his first West End audience, standing on the top of a stepladder, wearing army boots, a string vest and a Nazi helmet, and singing 'When I Was a Young Man, My Vest Was Always Dirty.'

To broaden his opportunities, Gambon enrolled in an improvisational acting class run by William Gaskill and George Devine at the Royal Court. When Gaskill moved to the Old Vic as an associate director later that year, he was instrumental in getting Gambon an audition with Olivier, who was gathering actors for the first National Theatre company. Gambon's story of his audition, which is recounted in one of the conversations in this book, is one of his (and my) favourites, and, as with all such tales, he is fond of embroidering it for dramatic effect. But, having been accepted for the new National, Gambon seemed stalemated, and Olivier suggested that he would find greater opportunity in a provincial repertory company like the Birmingham Rep where, 40 years earlier, Olivier had served his own apprenticeship. Olivier telephoned Birmingham. With Olivier's recommendation, Gambon was accepted, and almost immediately began playing larger roles. Then came an event that changed the course of his career – the first time he took advantage of a demanding assignment and was seen by those best able to help him.

It was 1968, and as the climax of the season he played the title role in *Othello*. Iago was played by Brian Cox, a Scotsman six years his junior. Cox was being considered for the leading role in a new BBC adventure series called *The Borderers*, and had been telling Gambon so for months. One day Cox informed Gambon that *The Borderers* people would be at that evening's performance. In a sudden twist of fate, the producers offered the television role not to Cox but to Gambon. After finishing the season in Birmingham, Gambon swung into *The Borderers*, learned to ride a horse and changed his billing from Mike Gambon to the more formal Michael Gambon. *The Borderers* became a popular series. In 1970 he began a season with the Royal Shakespeare Company and then played a Member of Parliament in a second TV series, *The Challengers*. Another actor in that series, Eric Thompson, was moving into directing. Casting *The Norman Conquests*, a new Alan Ayckbourn trilogy, he enlisted Gambon to play the role of Tom, the vet. That proved to be the first of several breakthroughs: Simon Gray's *Otherwise Engaged*, and onward to *Galileo*, *King Lear* and *Antony and Cleopatra* – and, of course, *The Singing Detective*.

The role in *The Singing Detective* called for Gambon to be immobilised much of the time in a hospital bed suffering from a severe skin condition. For such a highly physical actor, that might seem to impose restraint. The opposite turned out to be true. He was forced to use other resources. 'His face was a battlefield in that bed,' said the author, Dennis Potter. 'He used his eyes in the most amazing fashion.' From behind his ravaged mask of a face, his eyes and his voice spoke with authority as a man afflicted but who is carrying on with a clownish spirit.

Potter observed, 'When he was in maximum make-up, with all the sores and lesions on his face, he wouldn't eat with the rest of the cast and crew in the hospital dining room. It was as though he actually had the disease and didn't like being seen like that.' Potter credited Gambon with a lack of self-consciousness in performance, in contrast to other English actors. 'They seem as if they were a micro-millimetre away from themselves, looking at themselves,' he said. 'He's a very un-actory actor. He's also a very shy man. You wouldn't be surprised to encounter him in a Dickens novel, wearing patent-leather shoes and sitting on a high stool, and yet doing amazing things when he locks the office door. There's something of that that comes out in his acting.'

In performance, he is more than a chameleon. There is something chimerical about his role-playing. Just as his face is an empty canvas ready to be filled with expressiveness, his body seems to alter its shape in performance. Although by his own description he is 'a big-boned bloke,' he seemed small when he played a timid soul in Ayckbourn's *Man of the Moment*. Yet as Eddie Carbone he was a titan striding the waterfront. In *The Singing Detective*, as the psoriasis-ravaged Philip Marlow, in dream sequences he leaves his hospital bed to become a dashing and dapper singer. And as Lear he seemed physically to shrink into old age. Trying to explain this immense malleability, Peter Hall said, 'He seems to be able to turn his sense of physical bulk on and off at will. He is like those great actors of France and Germany who are marinated in every kind of classical role and seem able to do anything . . . Fate gave him genius, but he uses it as a crafts-man. He can switch off different areas of his personality and remake himself. Most actors bring the part to themselves. In some curious way, Michael takes himself to the part.'

That is, I think, an important clue to Gambon's art. Where other actors might try to disguise the faults of a character, he accepts them as integral traits. And he demonstrated as Galileo that he is one of those rare actors who are capable of personifying creativity. It would be easy – and accurate – to say that he is a natural, but there is more to his acting than that. Despite a lack of intellectualism, he has a probing mind, the keenest powers of observation, and the integrity of an Old Master portraitist. He feels his way into a role and then takes an imaginative leap into another man's psyche. Like Richardson, he subscribes to the theory that acting is 'like being in a dream.'

When Gambon arrives for rehearsal, he is unencumbered by the excess baggage of memories drawn from life. Instead, he has a sense of selective recall. Ideas and images 'cook inside' him. Describing Gambon's process, John Dexter once said, 'Until he has solved all the practical problems – how to move, how to speak, whether to turn on the right foot or the left – that volcano of poetry can't erupt.'

Gambon's characterisations evolve slowly. Ayckbourn said that the first reading of *A Chorus of Disapproval* was 'the worst I've ever had in a play of mine,' and added, 'Michael reversed or inverted every line and read in a sort of Irish-Indian accent, which was the nearest he got to Welsh at that point.' When Gambon finally worked his way into the role, it was a bravura comic performance.

In Ayckbourn's *Man of the Moment*, Gambon played Douglas Beechey, a mild-mannered bank clerk who rose to an act of heroism by disarming a thief during a robbery and was then subjected to manipulation by the media. The robber served a prison sentence, but on his release became a famous author and television celebrity, while the heroic bank clerk faded into obscurity. After 17 years, the two are brought together for a television reunion. Gambon could have played either role but chose Douglas. He was marvellous as the character, playing him with a sweet sincerity that made one think of Chaplin, or of Alec Guinness in his early movies. For his role, Gambon won an Olivier Award as best actor in a comedy, one of a series of award-winning performances. The day after I saw *Man of the Moment*, I met Gambon for the first time, and we began talking about acting and about actors.

In personal and practical terms, his work is 'a compulsion'. He once said to me, 'I don't really like it. I *have* to do it.' And he added, 'Fundamentally, acting is a deep process of showing off in front of a thousand people, dressing up in costumes and saying, "Look at me." Actors are show-offs, bigheaded bastards, egomaniacs. I can't think of any other reason they act. Can you?' When I suggested that actors were interpretative artists, he laughed loudly and said, 'Well, yeah, but they're still bigheaded bastards.' I drew a parallel between actors and musicians, mentioning Arthur Rubinstein as an exemplar of the interpretative artist, and Gambon suddenly became assertive about what he considers to be the most important difference. 'It didn't matter what Rubinstein looked like,' he said. 'He had a piano, which is a solid thing – and this great skill. He was lucky. Actors just have this.' He pointed at himself. 'And it's fuck-all they can do about it.'

In a crowd, he might be the last person you would identify as an actor. As Dennis Potter said, 'He's a bit like an old pair of shoes.' Once, when he was rehearsing a television play, Gambon drove to the studio and had trouble finding a parking space. A man who seemed to be in charge of the car park at the studio directed him to a space and said that he would take care of him from that day on. Gambon accepted this as one of the perks of celebrity. The last day of rehearsals, he got out of his car and snapped the script of the play down on the roof. The man asked him what that was. He said, 'The script of the play we're rehearsing.' 'The play?', the man said in astonishment. 'Are you an actor? I thought you were the fucking maintenance man.'

No wonder that when Gambon went to Buckingham Palace to be made a Commander of the Empire in 1990, Queen Elizabeth whispered to her equerry before the investiture, 'What's it for?' The aide whispered back, 'Acting.' A decade later when Prince Charles knighted him and Gambon joined the august company of Sirs, there was no doubt about his profession. Charles knew who he was. He had seen him perform and his movie roles had brought him a wider audience. Still, he cherishes anonymity and is not always recognised in public. And when he goes to meetings and conventions with other gunsmiths and gun collectors, he is just another bloke. Well, almost.

Though he is six-feet tall, he seems larger; he has a barrel chest and a tendency to put on weight. Because his hair is thin and receding, his face seems quite broad. He often wears a moustache, of varying dimensions and styles, and sometimes a full beard. His eyes, which are grey, are heavy-lidded; in repose, he can look faintly Oriental. To those who know him well or watch him closely, his most notable features are his long arms and large hands. He has long, tapered fingers that look as if they had been sculptured in ivory. He uses his hands gracefully, whether he is lighting a cigarette, duelling in a stage battle, or engraving the handle of an antique weapon. One of his special talents is 'finger-walking'. His fingers become the equivalent of hand puppets, marching across a pub table – traditionally at the Dirty Duck in Stratford – swaggering, stumbling, collapsing, depending on which actor he is mimicking.

Searching for ways to describe Gambon in performance, critics have reached for animal imagery, comparing him to a lion, a bear, a gorilla, and, in one bizarre instance, a giant sea anemone. Amenable even to the anemone, Gambon supposed that that was a reference to his long arms. His feet are also large. One is size 12, the other twelve and a half; both are narrow and impossible to fit. In London, he generally has his shoes handmade by a bootmaker. 'If you looked at him walking along the street, at first glimpse you would think he had a couple of pounds of lead weight in his feet,' Potter said. 'Yet there's this nimbleness, and an incredible lightness.' Gambon moves with a long, loping walk that leads him, when he is climbing stairs, to take two steps at a time. His hands and his feet become essential aspects of his performance. He says that if he had been born again, he would have been a ballet dancer – and one feels the glimmer of truth behind the desire.

The cliché about English actors – that they are all head and no heart – is belied by Gambon: he projects a rugged masculinity and intensity. In his acting style, he is a bridge between England and the United States. As has been said about Marlon Brando, he is unpredictable in performance, bringing with him a sense of surprise and even of danger. One never knows what he might do next, in either comedy or tragedy. Adrian Noble, who directed him in both *King Lear* and *Antony and Cleopatra*, compares him to Edmund Kean, as in Coleridge's famous description: 'To see him act is like reading Shakespeare by flashes of lightning.'

There is, of course, another, antic side to Gambon. He can be a cut-up, a clown and a corpser breaking up other actors onstage. He loves to laugh and is a great practical joker, and there are many examples of his outrageous humour throughout this book. Despite his reputation for reserve and his dislike of interviews, he is an expansive talker and anecdotalist. Our conversations are filled with long stories about the actor's life and with his laughter at remembered moments of tomfoolery. As his fellow actors know, he is also great company, and in the British tradition, he is a spinner of tales and a dispenser – and inventor? – of yarns about the theatre. As he freely confesses, when it comes to telling stories, he instinctively elaborates. He is certainly a self-dramatiser. Legends have grown up around him, even more than with Richardson (his eccentricities) or Gielgud (his 'bricks'). In several cases, variant, even contradictory, versions of Gambon stories appear in this book. Which is true? That's for him to know and for us to enjoy.

Onstage, he has a low boredom level. He quickly tires of playing the same role, and he is known for varying his performances, which is why theatregoers are always encouraged to see him early in the run of a play. He does not like long runs, and in recent years has managed to avoid them. Because of Gambon's behaviour in performance, he has had problems with some directors, who feel that he is undisciplined. He is disciplined, but he is always looking for ways to interest and amuse himself. Deborah Warner says it is the responsibility of the director to keep him interested (but what happens when the director is away?). He owns up to this failing, but there is something unnatural about being expected to repeat a performance over and over again. Gambon does not repeat himself, and some of his alterations – according to mood, accident or audience reaction – are not observable. They are known to him and perhaps to no-one else.

Despite his apparent lightheartedness, he takes acting very seriously, as he does his other activities, beginning with his work as a gunsmith, in which he can refine a problem to a millionth of an inch. He is concerned that mechanical engineering is a lost art and he is a firm believer in the necessity of man being able to control his environment and to repair the instruments in his daily life. He wears a non-digital watch, and can fix watches as well as cars. His dream project is to create an entire pre-computer precision workshop, a kind of private museum of the way things worked in the 1950s. One could certainly draw a parallel between his mechanical inventiveness and his brilliance as an actor.

Everything in his life is self-made. Onstage, he is a master of the specific move or gesture, yet always retains a sense of the broad picture. Repeatedly he says that he has little to say about acting, and less to say about how he acts. He could not imagine himself teaching acting, except perhaps by example. In the middle of an attempt at analysis, he will stop and apologise and declare that what he is saying is made up on the spur of the moment. Actually he knows a great deal about acting and about the geneology of actors. In his own way, he is a kind of historian of his profession: if only he could have studied Kean and Macready as he did Olivier. It is fascinating to hear him talk about acting, how he can stand back and visualise how he will look onstage in juxtaposition to the other actors. Although he acts with his intuition, he is also a finely detailed craftsman and he has eloquent command of his body and voice. Despite his protestations, he knows exactly what he does onstage.

Previous books in this series have consisted of my conversations with playwrights (Harold Pinter, Tom Stoppard, Samuel Beckett and Arthur Miller), three of whom – Stoppard is the exception – have provided Gambon with some of his most challenging roles. Admittedly, the actor's art is more nebulous and more difficult to characterise, especially for someone who is self-taught like Gambon. The key to him is, of course, in his acting. I have seen almost all his major performances in London and at Stratford-upon-Avon. With the exception of several television roles – most notably, of course, in *The Singing Detective* – his best performances have been on the stage.

As Gambon's career continued to flourish, I wrote a profile about him for the *New Yorker* magazine. Under the title 'The Complete Actor,' it appeared in the issue of 28 January 1991. In the years that followed, we have met frequently in London and in New York, often informally for lunch or dinner. During this time, he has expanded his repertoire in roles as varied as the wealthy restaurateur in Hare's *Skylight*, the seedy, manipulative Davies in a revival of Pinter's *The Caretaker*, and as the self-centered but regretful father who has cloned his son in Caryl Churchill's *A Number*. Ralph Richardson was right: he is The Great Gambon.

MEL GUSSOW
January 2004

'Actors and actresses always required for near-professional productions'

advertisement in a London theatre magazine

I had written to Larry Dalzell, Michael Gambon's agent, telling him that I wanted to write a profile of Gambon for the New Yorker, *and the actor had agreed to spend as much time with me as possible over a period of two weeks. At the time, he was appearing in the West End in Alan Ayckbourn's* Man of the Moment, *and our conversations would be slotted in between performances. We met for the first time in Dalzell's office in Covent Garden. Gambon was wearing his banker's suit – blue, double-breasted – and a red tie (and white socks). Keeping in English character, he was carrying an umbrella. We walked briskly to the Frère Jacques restaurant. As we talked at lunch, he seemed as eager to please as Douglas Beechey, his character, an accidental hero, in* Man of the Moment. *That summer he was doing a double-header of plays at Ayckbourn's theatre in Scarborough:* Othello *and a revival of Ayckbourn's* Taking Steps. *It was immediately evident that he was a good storyteller but did not feel comfortable offering theories or analyses of acting. He began with an apology.*

GAMBON: I've always had a reluctance to talk about acting. My acting is just instinctive. Quite simply, I read a play a lot. I have to find out what the man looks like, and what he's wearing – and then everything else seems to fit into place. I'm not saying it's not work, but I don't overcomplicate things, and I don't do research.

MG: Olivier often said that he began preparing for a role with a nose and an accent. It was very important to him to know the look and the sound of his characters. Do you go through any similar process?

GAMBON: I just say what the author wrote and put my own thing on top of it. I'm thinking about Othello now. I'm totally obsessed with what he looks like. Should he have a shaved head? I've got to play this terribly difficult part and here I am worried about this, but it's important to know what this man looks like. I've been thinking about exotic things: should he wear a ponytail, which he would flick when he went berserk?

MG: Is hair more important to you than other aspects of a character's appearance?

GAMBON: No, but Othello's hair worries me because he's a black man. I have to make up black or brown or whatever. As I have little hair myself, I think, does he wear a wig? You can't get away with a wig in a tiny theatre. So what do I do? You know, Alan Ayckbourn doesn't want much acting in his play. I know that's a strange thing to say, but he said it to me last night. He doesn't want an actor making comments on the character he's playing by adding things of his own. He wants a purity of the play. That's very difficult to achieve. When we were rehearsing, it was quite easy to do. It's just in the long run, after three months, if the play begins to slide, all sorts of things start to be introduced. The difficulty is being truthful without pleading for laughs or doing funny business. It's a matter of taste and discretion. On matinees I usually hook up my trousers a bit to have a funnier walk. He told me last night not to do that. He said, 'That gesture is too expansive. He's not an expansive man.'

MG: The last performance of yours that I saw before this was in the movie, *The Cook, the Thief, His Wife and Her Lover*, which is the other side of the planet.

GAMBON: Grotesque. That was good fun.

MG: More fun than this?

GAMBON: Yes, because you could do what you liked. You can't do what you like in this play. You can't just play around with it, because the whole thing would collapse. Ayckbourn's plays are built like clocks. They're very precise and if anyone goes away on a limb, the play shakes, whereas in *The Cook, the Thief*, Peter Greenaway [the director] let us do what we wanted to do. When that gang of murderers was around that table, we were throwing food. There wasn't any reverence for the text.

MG: And for an actor, that's a relief?

GAMBON: It's just fun, yes, it's fun playing big villains like that. It's like being a child really. It was like letting a bunch of 12-year-olds play because that's what we turned into – anarchy.

MG: How much are your performances self-directed?

GAMBON: I usually find my own way through things.

MG: But you've worked with some very strong directors: John Dexter, Adrian Noble.

GAMBON: I've always felt uneasy with directors and I regard them, with the exception of Alan, maybe as enemies. I'm rather frightened of them. I was always frightened of John Dexter. He was quite a formidable man, so you always worked to please him in case he shouted at you. But I quite like being pushed into a corner like John used to do. He would drive you through the play, make you work. I like working with Alan because I put the father figure on him.

MG: He's not much older than you are. But he's the father and you're the son?

GAMBON: Yes. I don't think he'd like to hear me say that.

MG: From the first, you've been able to play characters older than yourself.

GAMBON: I suppose that's because I've got a deep voice and I'm rather heavy, so I tend to endow things with more weight, which makes me look older. But most of the parts I've played in the past 10 years – apart from King Lear – have been about my own age. I make them look a bit older, maybe. I've never played 'juve' parts, except in my first big TV series in the late '60s.

MG: Years ago when I talked to Olivier, he took credit for discovering you, saying that you were one of his 'old boys' at the Old Vic, adding that you had become 'a very important actor.'

GAMBON: We all loved him. He was great. I asked him for better parts, and he said, 'No, I can't give them to you. If I were you, I'd leave.' And he picked up the phone and got me a job at the Birmingham Rep, which was a very nice thing to do.

MG: Would you have wanted to stay at the Old Vic at that point?

GAMBON: I don't think so. There was nothing for me. The men who were playing the parts I wanted – Derek Jacobi, John Stride, Bob Stephens – were firmly established, so there was no way I could do the jump. Tony Hopkins managed it and stayed there with Olivier and played leading roles.

MG: Could we go back to when you started? You were born in Dublin, then moved to London and began working as an engineer.

GAMBON: Precision engineering. I left school when I was 15. I got a job in a factory as a tea boy. Making tea and running round and sweeping up. After six months they put you on an apprenticeship where you sign indentures for five years. I stayed there until I was 21.

MG: Were those difficult years?

GAMBON: No, I loved it. I've always been obsessed by it,

still am. I do an awful lot of work with my hands, and I find it's great therapy. Sometimes it worries me because it becomes more important than acting when you're in a long run.

MG: What do you make with your hands?

GAMBON: I restore antique firearms – English 18th-century guns. I've been a gun collector since I was a kid. So, having engineering skills, I've applied them over the years to these things. I've taught myself. I've also had experience as an engraver. I engrave and inlay in steel. I taught myself most of the skills required for that sort of work, and I have a large range of things I do with wood and metal.

MG: You never went back to school after 15?

GAMBON: No, that was the end.

MG: Where did you learn what you know?

GAMBON: Being in the theatre is a good education. Being at the RSC is like being at a university, I should imagine. The rehearsals become like tutorials. When people sit around and discuss the play and literature, it just rubs off on you.

MG: Many actors went to university.

GAMBON: Most of them. So I've learned from them. They're all able to talk wonderfully, but the technique and skill of staging a play sometimes eludes them, so you have five actors standing in a straight line playing a scene.

MG: The physical side of acting is important to you, the differences in how characters walk.

GAMBON: The walks just come with the learning of the character in rehearsal. They just seem to grow out of what the man's saying, what his attitude is. Eddie Carbone [in *A View from the Bridge*] is working on ships and lifting great heavy weights, so I thought that's the way he'd walk.

MG: After you finished your indenture, why didn't you stay with engineering?

GAMBON: When I was 17 or 18, I started acting in the evenings with an amateur dramatic society, in Erith in Kent. There was a little theatre in the High Street, and it said outside, 'Backstage Help Required.' I went in just out of curiosity – I've always been quite a curious person – and I started helping them build sets.

MG: At that point, you hadn't seen any plays?

GAMBON: I'd never been to a play. I didn't know what a play was. I watched one and realised it was the same as what James Dean was doing down the road on the screen. [At other times, he would say that it was Marlon Brando that he had seen in films.] They gave me a few bit parts. I went, *varoom!* I thought, Jesus, this is for me. I want to be an actor.

MG: What were some of your first roles?

GAMBON: I was in Peter Shaffer's *Five Finger Exercise* and *The Old Curiosity Shop*, plays like that. I started buying theatre magazines, one called *Amateur Stage*, and in the back of it, there was an advert for Unity Theatre. It said, 'Actors and actresses always required for near-professional productions.' They were up in Kings Cross, Camden Town. I went along there. They'd do a six-week run playing only Friday, Saturday and Sunday. I was an apprentice at Vickers Amstrong. I was around 18. I'd get the train up to London after I'd finish work, and I'd rehearse with Unity Theatre. I was unaware that it was a left-wing political theatre. I also worked at another amateur theatre called the Tower Theatre, in Islington. Finally the first job I ever got paid for was a Sunday night production at the Royal Court. Then I wrote letters to companies and finally got a walk on part with the Edwards-MacLiammóir company in Ireland.

MG: To get that job, you lied about your experience?

GAMBON: I was a terrible liar. I wrote a letter to Hilton Edwards and said I was flying to New York and I was passing through Dublin. Could I come and see him? So I went to

Dublin and he said, 'What have you played?' and I told him I'd played Marchbanks in the West End. He didn't even question it. He said, 'Well, I can't offer you any good parts but would you play the Second Gentleman of Cyprus [in *Othello*]?' To say that to a man who's just played Marchbanks in the West End, he must have known I was bullshitting. I said, 'Yes, I would love to.' Then he said, rehearsals would start on October 1st, and that was it. I did that and we played in the Dublin Theatre Festival and then we did a European tour. Then I came back to London and got myself a little part in a play at the Mermaid Theatre and I understudied in a Spike Milligan show in the West End. During the days, I managed to get in an acting course at the Royal Court, which was run by Bill Gaskill and George Devine. It was an advanced sort of improvisation class.

MG: That was the first acting that you studied?

GAMBON: Yes. Improvisation and mask work. I went there for six months. Then Bill Gaskill was appointed an associate director of the new National Theatre, which was about to open, and so I managed to get an audition. That was how I got in there, and since then I've never done anything else.

MG: When you first started to act, what did it mean to you?

GAMBON: I've always loved the whole romantic thing with the theatre, the smell of it and all that. That sounds a bit coddish, but it's true. I remember when I did that first Sunday night play at the Royal Court [*The Sea at Dauphin*, in which he was the only white actor in a company of black actors], I just couldn't stop walking through the stage door. I'd go in and find some excuse to come out. Then I'd go round Sloane Square and go in again, just hoping someone would see me walking through the stage door. It sounds bizarre.

MG: It sounds stagestruck.

GAMBON: Yes, totally stagestruck! I still am. That's what I've always been.

MG: Did any of your friends go into acting?

GAMBON: Oh no, not at all. I used to mention it to people at the factory where I was working and they would just laugh or walk away. I quickly learned not to talk about it.

MG: In the English tradition, one goes through Cambridge and RADA.

GAMBON: Colin Blakely never went to drama school. He had much the same sort of amateur theatre life in Northern Ireland, and he didn't become an actor professionally until he was nearly 30. He was in his father's business.

MG: Your father died while you were performing *Macbeth?*

GAMBON: He died on the first night. I was doing *Macbeth* at Billingham, up north.

MG: Tell me about your siblings.

GAMBON: I have a brother and a sister who's a housewife. My brother is a manager of a chemical company. They have nothing to do with the theatre at all. There was no background of acting in the family. When I was 11 or 12, I was obsessed by the Church. I was an altar boy in the Catholic Church. I think I did that mainly because of the dressing up. I had to learn the whole text in Latin and serve on the altar at six o'clock in the morning. I used to love that. I've always had a bit of a need to get up and display myself.

MG: In order to join the Old Vic, you had to audition for Olivier.

GAMBON: That's a story I tell people. I was so green about the theatre and the history of the theatre and about him that I did Richard III for him for the audition. And I hadn't a clue. When I look back on it now, I shake with embarrassment.

MG: You did his role?

GAMBON: I never knew he had done it. He said, 'What are you going to do?' I said, 'Richard III.' He said, 'Which part?'

I said, 'Richard III.' He said, 'I know. Which part?' He was fooling. He said, 'Which part? Catesby? Buckingham?' I said, 'No. Richard III.' He said, 'The King?' I said, 'Yes.' He said, 'You have the fucking cheek.' Then I was genuinely frightened. I said, 'Oh, I'm sorry.' He said, 'No, no, you do it.' I immediately started. He said, 'No, no. You're standing too close to me. You can't start doing that famous part leaning over me.' He was sitting at a table. 'You've got to walk away from me. I've got to see you in full perspective. Go to the back of the hall and do it there.' So I went up the hall. There were columns holding the roof up. I got to the last one. I dived for the column. I don't know what came over me. I spun round and I started the speech, but as I went around, I ripped the whole of my hand. A nail in the column went straight through – blood, pfff. He said, 'No. Stop, stop. You're not dying are you? What's happened? We have to get a doctor. Where's a doctor, where's a doctor?' He gave me his handkerchief. He wrapped my hand. 'I'll do it now,' I said. He said, 'No, no. This is appalling.' I said, 'But I have to do the audition.' He said, 'You go away and we'll be in touch with you.' So I got the job.

MG: How did you feel about Olivier as an actor?

GAMBON: I love his sort of acting. He really went for effect, didn't he? When he did his curtain call in *Othello*, he'd walk down the centre of the stage, and he would put his hand on his heart. The house would be screaming and he would put his other arm up like that and then drop it. An actor in the wings said to him, 'What's all that shit that you're doing, Larry?' He said, 'I'll tell you one thing. You'll never do it.' Which was cutting, but true. He knew he was a great actor. He had all the attributes. He was compact. When you looked at him on the stage, there was nothing out of proportion. He always had his shoulders built out a bit, and he had very narrow hips. He was like an acting machine; he was built for acting.

MG: Did you feel that way about Gielgud or Richardson?

GAMBON: Not Gielgud. I've never had any contact with him at all, but I certainly felt that way about Ralph Richardson, although I didn't see him as an heroic actor like Olivier. Sir Ralph was a demonstrator of acting, wasn't he? If he had to fall over in a play, he'd show you, like in slow motion, how he was falling. He was like a Brechtian actor, really, slightly removed from his part.

MG: He called you The Great Gambon.

GAMBON: I think he thought I was a circus act. I was in a play with him once. It was a flop. It ran for three weeks in the West End. It was a dreadful, dreadful play called *Alice's Boys*, a spy thriller. It had a very good cast and we all did it because *he* was in it. The greatest actor in the world was in this play, and we all agreed to be in it. And of course it was a disaster because we didn't read the play. He stood in the wings one night with an empty house and he said to me, 'Oh, dear, it's terrible, isn't it?' and I said, 'Yes, it is.' He said, 'It's awful. In the old days, nice people used to come to the theatre. Now they send their cooks.'

I said, 'Why are you doing this play, Sir Ralph?' He said, 'Because in the opening scene, I have to do needlework.' I said, 'That's the only reason you accepted it?' He said, 'Why did *you* accept it?' I said, 'You were in it.' It was a terrible play. I bet one of the actors two hundred pounds that it would run for six months. But it ran for two weeks.

MG: That was the only time you acted with him?

GAMBON: Yes, but I knew him quite well because he was always at the National when I was there in different shows. I used to sit with him a lot.

MG: Would he tell you about acting?

GAMBON: He would say that acting was like being in a dream. I bought him a box as a present. He kept this box on his table in his dressing room. One day he opened it and inside was a rotten, rotten old black pill, like you'd give a sick horse. He said, 'I want you to have this.' And I said, 'What is it?' And he said, 'It's a pill. You'd better take it now.' I said, 'What is it?' And he said, 'I don't know. I have no idea what it is.' I said, 'Well, how can I take it?' He said, 'With water.' 'Yeah, but how can I take it without knowing what it is?' He said, 'Well, that pill was prescribed for me by a doctor – in 1946.' 'So he prescribed that pill, just one pill?' He said, 'I think so. I can't remember. I'm getting angry, sitting here, talking to you like this. Will you please take the pill?' So, being rather meek, I took it. I don't know what that's got to do with acting.

MG: Perhaps it turned you into an actor.

GAMBON: Maybe it was an acting pill.

MG: So Richardson's advice to a young actor was to take a pill. Did Olivier give you any advice?

GAMBON: Well, he was always talking. I understudied Colin Blakely in *The Crucible*, and one day we did an understudy rehearsal for Sir Laurence so that he could see how we were getting on. I played Proctor, and at the end of it, he said, 'Very good, but don't listen to people.' I said, 'What do you mean?' He said, 'Don't listen to the other actors in the play. You know your lines, don't you? You know your cue lines.' I said yes. He said, 'So you know your cue is coming up and you know your own lines. There's no need to listen so hard while they're talking.' I've never been able to decipher that. Maybe he meant I should be more naturalistic and not be locked into that.

MG: Did you work with Olivier onstage?

GAMBON: I was in his *Othello* and I was in *The Recruiting Officer* and a Feydeau farce.

MG: Is there something to be learned from working with . . .

GAMBON: With actors like that? Well, I suppose it just rubs off on you watching them working because you find there's no secret.

MG: There's no secret?

GAMBON: Yes. They're not doing something that you don't do. They stand in the rehearsal room the way you do, with their script open. They stand in the wings the way you do. We all used to watch Sir Laurence like hawks. But he'd stand in the wings like everybody else and walk like everybody else. The secret was something extra he had, which I suppose is acting, isn't it? When he'd go out on the stage, he knew how to do it.

MG: I assume you had a similar reaction to Marlon Brando. You did the movie *A Dry White Season* because you wanted to work with him?

GAMBON: Oh, yes! I just wanted to be in the same room as him.

MG: What did you learn from Brando?

GAMBON: Oh, I just learned that he was a wonderful bloke. I learned that he wasn't Brando, The Method Actor. We got there on the first day and I had eight lines or something. He wasn't at all concerned with Method acting. He said, 'I want a surgical boot.' They were supposed to start shooting that day. He said, 'I want a surgical boot with a big platform sole that lifts my foot three inches off the ground.' [*He demonstrates by mimicking Brando's voice and clumping his foot on the floor.*] The director said, why? And he said, 'Well, I just want it.' And then he said, 'I want a walking stick.' He got the boot, the walking stick and a little pair of glasses. He's just as concerned with his looks as Laurence Olivier was. So that's what I learned. When Brando is in a film studio with a camera on him, he is able to relax. He was constantly fooling about. The director would say 'Action', and he'd say, 'What's that?' It was four days of joy, lots of laughter. He reminded me of a gorilla. Gorillas examine things very closely. [*He picks up a glass and examines it, as a gorilla might.*] If you go to the zoo, they're constantly picking things up from the floor or they're looking at their coat. They're always interested in everything around them. Brando reminded me of that in the studio. That's partly due to the fact that he doesn't want to meet anybody's eyes – in case he has to say hello to them. He would constantly be at his desk when he was shooting – always fiddling with things. It wasn't a difficult part he had to play. He just did it because he approves of the cause. Donated his fee to Soweto, or something. I'm just overawed by people like that. Stars.

MG: Is there anyone else?

GAMBON: Oh, Robert De Niro. I would walk barefoot to Palestine to meet him. I think he's brilliant. I've seen all his movies. I know nothing about him at all. The less people know about you, the better it is. The more they know about you, the more it fucks up your job. If you walk on the stage and they say, 'Oh, there's the man who restores antique guns' . . . if they know nothing about you, then the canvas can become easier to paint on.

MG: After I saw *Man of the Moment*, I thought about other actors who might have been able to play your part – perhaps, years ago, Alec Guinness would have had a shot at it.

GAMBON: Yes, absolutely. It helped me to think of him. I've seen all his films. I think they're wonderful. I don't know why he doesn't do more. Maybe he just got fed up with acting. Stage acting is such hard work. There's nothing wrong with hard work, but it's wearing on the legs and the lungs. But whenever I've been away from the stage for a bit and done television, after three months I'm pining for it again.

MG: How do you feel about the audience?

GAMBON: It's very difficult to play this play now every night because the audiences have changed subtly. We're getting more of a coach audience, so the coughing is getting worse. Some nights it's like a chest hospital. And you can't pace the scene, so then you really hate them. I think most actors hate the audience. Some wouldn't dare admit it.

MG: Some might feel nurtured by the response.

GAMBON: Yes. If they really help, it's wonderful.

MG: Some actors like the direct response in terms of laughter.

GAMBON: I've seen some actors who enter into a conspiracy with the audience. That's not good . . . It's a skilled job, acting. It's a matter of judging the evening and not boring people sitting out there. That's crude, but it's part of the process.

MG: Have you ever felt that you were boring audiences?

GAMBON: Some nights, particularly with Alan's plays. The audience comes to see them because Ayckbourn's reputation is that he is a comedy writer. They sit there and laugh. When Alan's serious themes start coming, you can feel the audience getting restless. That's when you get nervous about boring them. In the first two months of a play where you get all the theatre nuts in, that's no problem, because they're on to it straight away. But the average theatregoer sees Ayckbourn to have a laugh.

MG: You prefer then to have a run of two months.

GAMBON: I think three months is ideal, but it's financially impossible.

MG: What's the longest run you've had?

GAMBON: I've done a year, every night, eight times a week, in *Otherwise Engaged*. After six months, you're just dead. There's no originality, it's just like repeating.

MG: That was the first time I saw you onstage. That was a turning point for you.

GAMBON: Yes, but the real turning point was 1974 when I did *The Norman Conquests*. I got good reviews for that very placid vet, and that changed my career a bit. I got to know Ayckbourn, I met Michael Codron [the producer] and Harold Pinter, who cast me in *Otherwise Engaged* [which Pinter directed]. Through Harold, I met Peter Hall, and after that came *Betrayal* two years later, and then from *Betrayal* came *Galileo*.

MG: How did you get the part in *The Norman Conquests*?

GAMBON: It just came out of the blue. I had done a TV series [*The Challengers*] with an actor-director called Eric Thompson, who's Emma Thompson's father, and he was just starting a career as a director, and he managed to get the job of directing the three *Norman Conquests* at Greenwich. When we finished the series, I was going up to Edinburgh to play *The Doll's House* at the Lyceum Theatre. Eric rang me up and said, 'Do you want to play this vet in these three plays?' I took the plays away with me and read them. I went from playing Ibsen in Edinburgh with Robert Kidd directing to rehearsing with Eric Thompson and Penny Keith and the other actors for *The Norman Conquests*. Then we went on in the West End for nine months.

MG: Had you played anything like it before?

GAMBON: I never played that sort of modern Ayckbourn man. And then I went straight into another Ayckbourn, *Just Between Ourselves*, playing the same type of man. That wasn't too successful. I went through *A Chorus of Disapproval*, playing that lunatic director and then *A Small Family Business* as that horrible businessman. It's the full circle. It's nice for people to know you have the ability to do complete opposites.

Did you see the one I did last year with Jack Lemmon [*Veterans' Day*]? Harold [Pinter] rang me up and said, 'I'm just about to play this part and I can't do it. Will you do it?' I had a four-month slot, and I flicked through the script. You quickly see there are just two people and I thought, Christ, that's wonderful. And then they say the other man is Jack

Lemmon. You go awww! And then you see the part you're playing, he's got long speeches where he talks about injustice, and it's quite dramatic. I said yes without reading it. But when you read the play through and stand up in the rehearsal room, it doesn't work. It wasn't a very happy experience. It was happy working with Jack Lemmon. In your avarice, you think, well, just two people in a big theatre – but of course it doesn't work like that. I turned up for the first read-through. Jack Lemmon didn't know who I was. He said, 'Where's Harold?' I said, 'He's not here.' After the read-through I said to him, 'Mr Lemmon, this play is a pile of crap.' He said, 'How dare you say that to me. I've come all the way from Los Angeles with my wife. We're staying at the Dorchester Hotel. I don't know who the fuck you are. I'm American, I'm optimistic. What are you doing the play for?' I apologised: I'm very, very sorry. But on the first night in the West End, we were in the wings ready to go on. He said, 'Michael, this play is a pile of crap.'

Jack had this theory about acting. In order to make it naturalistic, you should both speak at the same time. Like you would in a movie. Overlapping dialogue. So no-one ever heard a word. I'd be speaking to him and maybe an important part of the speech is at the end, but you would never hear it because he starts speaking before I got there. It was a mess. But good fun. And we finally went to the management, both of us together, and said, please take this off, it's unbearable. And so they did. Thank god.

Othello is completely knocking me out at the moment. There's not a lot you can do until you start rehearsing it, so these months leading up to that are very frustrating. This afternoon I'm going to see a shoemaker about making me some special Othello boots.

MG: Platform boots like Brando's?

GAMBON: No, but odd-looking ones. I'm going to get him to make me two pairs of special boots, the sort of thing you can

38

do what you like to them. You can cut holes, turn them into sandals, wrap things around them. I feel I have to get as much done as possible before I go up to Scarborough.

MG: Stepping into Othello's feet through his shoes?

GAMBON: Yes, yes. I'm there for four months, a month rehearsal, a month playing, then the plays are switched, so there's Shakespeare and then the Ayckbourn, then it's all over by December 18th. I've just signed a contract for a three-year deal to play Maigret, the French detective, on television. That would occupy me for four months of every year for the next three years, which is perfect. It means I can do theatre. I wouldn't have to speak in a French accent. I've read some of the novels. I'm looking forward to that. I like the idea of being a detective with a pipe and a hat.

MG: Like *The Singing Detective*. That certainly was a turning point.

GAMBON: Major! What a wonderful script. I've been so lucky in this business. Ian McKellen said to me the other day that one of my lucks was to do with writers. I've done Gray, Hampton, Pinter, Ayckbourn, all new plays.

MG: Why haven't you done a play in New York?

GAMBON: I've never been asked. I did a film in New York last year [*State of Grace*]. I had this call to go to New York first class. I'd never been there before. To play a gangster on the West Side of New York, with Sean Penn and Ed Harris. I found myself being shot with a machine gun out of the window of a car and then being blown back across the street, pulled on wires by the stunt man. The next day being in a basement in a scene playing cards, drinking scotch. That night I was on the plane back. I got a shock because they took half my money away in taxes.

MG: You like to fly planes.

GAMBON: I've got a pilot's licence. I go flying on Sundays. I always get lost, so I stick to one route, from Biggin Hill to

Ipswich. I hire it by the hour. I would have liked to have been an airline pilot. I like the idea of the white shirt and the gold stripes and the monstrous great aircraft and all the instruments and power. It's too late now, of course. I did voice-overs for Aer Lingus. I do lots of advertising voice-overs – commercials. Last year I said to the guy, 'Could you arrange for me to spend a day with a crew?' and they took me on a training flight in a Boeing 737, which was the highlight of the year.

MG: When you fly, do you dream about flying during a war?

GAMBON: No. I love to do really precision things. It's sort of armchair flying rather than leather-helmet-type flying.

MG: To do a little armchair analysis: when you fly a plane, you have ultimate control over what you do, although the plane could crash; whereas when you're acting you have no control.

GAMBON: Absolutely. Everything is very formalised.

MG: Would you prefer acting to be as formalised?

GAMBON: Probably. Flying an aircraft is very procedural. You can't do that with acting. Maybe that's why I do the engineering. I like the precision. If you measure something and it's got to be one-and-a-half inches, I like the fact that you can make it that size, not below or above by a half a millionth of an inch. I like practical solutions to acting problems.

Many of them are physical problems. Sometimes the reason a scene doesn't work between two actors is that they're in the wrong position. Geography of the stage is very important. I once understudied in a play that Dame Edith Evans was in. Her main preoccupation in the rehearsal room and all through the production was how close or how far away she was from the other actors. Richardson was a bit like that as well. He had this thing about the Laban theory of movement – that you have a bubble around you and the bubble is the same height as your head and the same width as your arms can stretch. And the bubble goes right round you. If anyone comes too near, it's like breaking into your space. It's like people who stand too close to you when they're talking to you.

MG: Does that mean one wouldn't touch Richardson on stage?

GAMBON: You would if the scene called for it. It's spatial awareness, isn't it? One day during rehearsals of *Lear*, Adrian Noble said I had a good spatial awareness. I had complained about the scene in which Lear banishes Cordelia. I said the daughters were too close to me. I couldn't explain why, but he took my point.

MG: What do you do on matinee days between shows?

GAMBON: After we come down on the matinee, I run round to the garage, where I've left my car. I have to get it out of the garage, drive it around the corner, park it at a single yellow line and stay there until half past six when the traffic warden's gone. I buy the evening paper, turn the news on and sit in the car.

MG: Why don't you leave it in the garage?

GAMBON: If I leave it in the garage, I can't get it out at night, I'm caught in a jam in the middle of Soho, and I sit in a queue of carbon monoxide. Come to the theatre tomorrow and I can leave it in the garage. We're down at 5.15, and we can have a cup of tea.

'I think I'm more the carthorse to Ian's racing thoroughbred'

At 5.30, after the matinee Gambon came out the stage door. He was dressed casually in ordinary trousers and a safari jacket. He guided me backstage to his dressing room. On the door was a sign, 'The Wanker of Suburbia.' The room was long, dim and not too comfortable-looking. He said we could sit there and send out for tea. I said that if he wanted to, we could rescue his car from the garage and he could park it on the street. Parking was a common bond between us. When I was in London I habitually drove to the theatre and parked my rented car on a single yellow line, which becomes a legal parking space after 6.30. He said that to avoid having his car clamped, he sometimes left a stethoscope by the window in the hope that he would be mistaken for a doctor. Somewhat sheepishly he led me to his nearby garage. We got into his BMW and he drove down Wardour Street until he found a space on a single yellow line. He was prepared to sit there until 6.30, and we began our conversation.

I said that this parking routine was demeaning for a star of his stature. Would Olivier have been sitting at the wheel of his car between performances? I told Gambon that he should have insisted that a space be reserved for him in the alley behind the theatre. One could sense that a parking space would be high on his list of perks.

GAMBON: I'm terribly sorry, Mel, that the interview is about parking cars.

MG: The only thing I'm worried about is that I'm keeping you from reading the newspaper. If you were, might not somebody stop by and say, 'I know him, but why is he sitting in a car reading a newspaper?'

GAMBON: Never. Sometimes you'll be walking along the street and people will recognise you. But they look away quick. There's no-one waiting at the stage door after the performance, although when I was in that play with Jack [Lemmon], we couldn't get out of the stage door. Some nights there were 50 to 100 people round it. Film stars. But not for us stage boys. For weeks on end, no-one comes back. You go out the stage door and there's no-one there. The first month, if you get good reviews, you're the talking point, but after that it goes into a lull and people forget you're on. Once you're up and running on the West End, you feel rather lost. In fact, you often meet people who say, 'What are you in now?'

MG: In a long run, do you find yourself wanting to improvise and change the lines?

GAMBON: Yes, there's a temptation to do that, but when you do you usually know you're doing the wrong thing, and you're only doing it for your own benefit to relieve the tedium.

MG: Once when you were acting with Scofield, you changed a line.

GAMBON: I was fooling about. It was Scofield's Othello, and I was Roderigo, and there was an actor in the company called Bill Sleigh. When Roderigo dies, he says, 'O, I am slain.' I don't know what comes over you. It's like the devil inside you. I just said, 'O, I am Bill Sleigh.'

MG: The audience wouldn't have known – unless there was an academic there with text in hand.

GAMBON: Paul Scofield knew.

MG: What did he say?

GAMBON: Oh, he loves that. He's a real joker. I've only done that one play with him. He didn't enjoy it. It wasn't his fault. It just didn't come to life. I thought it was all buttoned up. We were dressed in dark brown, which is depressing to start with, and he was dressed in doublet and hose. He couldn't move his body: he was like a man trussed up.

MG: Have you ever played Iago?

GAMBON: No. He's like a bee, bzzzz, all over the place, very light. I'm not terribly happy doing that sort of thing. I rather like heavier parts.

MG: I've seen Iago played as incarnate evil.

GAMBON: Someone asked Ralph Richardson about Iago once, about the motivation, and he said, 'Oh, he's a man who just got on the wrong bus.' The explanation for his behaviour is very simple, isn't it? He just hates the Moor, hates the black man. He's a racist, I think.

MG: Wasn't it Olivier who played into the supposedly latent homosexual side of Othello, with Richardson as his Iago?

GAMBON: And Richardson objected, didn't he?

MG: Olivier kissed Richardson.

GAMBON: Richardson said, 'If you kiss me again, I'll kill you.' [Laughter.] It's wonderful to create opposites. It would be wonderful if Othello and Iago were the closest buddies. That would help the belief in the story about the handkerchief – just a physical closeness, a touching, and then it would make the jealousy scenes more believable.

MG: It makes me think of other paired roles you've played, Vanya and Astrov, Lear and the Fool. You must have to build up a good relationship with the other actor. What happens if you don't?

GAMBON: It's just an unpleasant experience. I've been quite lucky. I've never really had much trouble in that way. Actors are very selfish by nature, and they have to be – to play leading parts. There's friction sometimes when two actors who play leading roles both grab for what they can get. There is a big competitive element in acting in the theatre. It's a bit like a boxing ring, and it's a healthy rivalry. When Tony [Sher] and I did the Fool and Lear, we got on like a house on fire. We used to improvise everything in rehearsals – being animals. And then the play opened, and I began to feel after a little while that the play was no longer King Lear's – because the Fool was so prominent. But I had to check myself, because that's not very creative.

MG: Sometimes in other productions, the Fool seems to disappear. You realise how few lines he has.

GAMBON: In David Hare's production [starring Anthony Hopkins as Lear], the Fool didn't exist. They were so frightened of the Fool being prominent that they almost got rid of him. Whenever Lear and the Fool had scenes together, they were on the opposite sides of the stage. It was weird.

MG: When you have two performances in one day, and the matinee does not go well, do you ever feel like packing it in and going home instead of doing the evening performance?

GAMBON: Yes, but you can't. Sometimes if you really smash a matinee, particularly in Shakespeare, the evening performance is brilliant. It's like putting yourself through a workout. At Stratford we did *King Lear* and *Antony and Cleopatra*.

MG: On the same day?

GAMBON: That was some day, that was. We'd do *King Lear* in the afternoon and then we'd nip up to The Other Place and do *Antony and Cleopatra*. Having gone through that, you were really on the ball. They were both Adrian [Noble, as director]. I really loved the *Antony*. It was a very, very simple production, and terribly fast. We played full text, but it came down early. We tore through it. It's one of my favourites. I love the scene when he talks to the moon and kills himself. The stars! Ah, well.

MG: How were you able to play Lear and Antony in one day?

GAMBON: It was easy. I don't like to see Lear played unless he's the proper age. That man is 80 years old. So we put a lot of make-up on, and wigs. And then with Antony you're playing a 40 year old. It was like a holiday. It's quite wonderful to play King Lear in the afternoon and then play Antony opposite Helen Mirren in the evening.

MG: The other way around wouldn't have been so easy.

GAMBON: No, we never did that.

MG: At the National, you did three plays in rep, *Tons of Money*, *A View from the Bridge* and *A Small Family Business*. Would you do two one day and one the next?

GAMBON: Sometimes we'd do two in one day, *Tons of Money* in the afternoon and *A View from the Bridge* in the evening. *A View from the Bridge* was a frightening thing to do. I found it difficult to get on that stage, particularly in the opening of Act Two, when he comes in drunk. That's the scene where he kisses the boy. I found that very hard to psych myself up, to get into the character of Eddie. Plus the fact you're playing a working-class man from New York. And it's about real people, not like Shakespeare. It's easier to step into the shoes of a king than to play someone who really lives and breathes and is modern. I think it's the only contemporary tragedy I've done.

MG: Didn't you feel closer to Eddie Carbone because of his working-class background?

GAMBON: If I saw the play, I'd probably feel sympathy for him. The other day at a platform question-and-answer session, someone asked Arthur Miller if it was right to feel sympathy for Eddie. I was relieved when Miller said yes, because he really doesn't know what he's doing, he's unaware of his own feelings about the girl. Talking about it now – I'd like to do it again.

Suddenly, the man in the car ahead of us, at a meter, pulled out and drove away. Gambon smoothly slid his car into the space. Satisfied with this manoeuvre, he had one last cigarette, discreetly holding it out the window. Then we walked back to the theatre, where we continued our talk. He said he was turning 50 that year.

GAMBON: It's like a milestone, being 50. My agent tells me I've been offered all sorts of parts in movies and I haven't been able to do them because of the theatre work. I'd like to make myself available.

MG: Could you compare working in theatre to working in movies and television?

GAMBON: I feel more at home in theatre. It's my country. The stage doesn't worry me. I feel as though I should be there, but I feel better in front of a camera now. *The Singing Detective* solved all those problems, to a certain extent.

MG: And as you say, you don't plan, things just fall your way?

GAMBON: Yes. It snowballs. The process is to say yes or no.

MG: Was there ever a temptation to say no? On the one hand, you have the satisfaction of being offered *Galileo* and *Lear*, but at the same time there might be some trepidation about suddenly playing the weightiest roles.

GAMBON: I've always been frightened of those big parts, but you've got to do them because they're the greatest parts ever written. If you shied away from them, why be an actor? I remember when I did *Galileo*, it was very, very successful and I got frightened about what I was going to do next. I was offered a couple of things which I turned down and finally I took *Much Ado About Nothing* at the National Theatre which wasn't good at all. But I think that was good for me. To have had a big hit with *Galileo*, and then the next play I did was a downer.

MG: What parts haven't you played that you want to play?

GAMBON: I'd like to play Falstaff one day. But that's about all I can think of.

MG: You missed *Hamlet.*

GAMBON: It would be wonderful to play Hamlet, but I've never been a Hamlet, never been built for Hamlet.

MG: What's 'a Hamlet'?

GAMBON: Hamlet is tall, thin. He's got a face that's chiselled on a statue. I think you have to be very young to play Hamlet. It's never come my way, but I suppose if someone offered it to me years ago, I would have done it.

MG: Macbeth?

GAMBON: I've done that. I enjoyed that. I didn't enjoy Coriolanus, because I couldn't get him. He keeps going on about his 'honour.' You've got to be a certain type of actor to play Coriolanus. You've got to be Alan Howard. You've got to have that patrician sort of hardness.

MG: Do you think of Alan Howard and Ian McKellen as the competition?

GAMBON: Alan Howard has everything a stage actor should have – a voice like metal. I saw Ian last night. Had a drink. I think of them as my contemporaries.

MG: As friendly rivals?

GAMBON: Yes. It's nice to have people who are going to grow old in this job with you. I don't know what I mean by that. I think you have to keep the tradition of theatre alive. I admire Ian for what he does because he works in the theatre constantly. He sees it as his life. Well, it is his life.

MG: Have you worked with him?

GAMBON: I walked on in Zeffirelli's *Much Ado About Nothing*, in which he played Claudio. That was in '64 or '65. I didn't really know him then. I saw him in his first professional play at the Belgrade Theatre in Coventry just after he left Cambridge University. I think I'm more a carthorse to Ian's racing thoroughbred. I don't meant carthorse in a derogatory way, but more of a heavyweight. He's lighter than me. I would say he's more in the Gielgud tradition.

MG: Did you ever see Orson Welles onstage?

GAMBON: No.

MG: I saw him do Lear in a wheelchair. He broke his leg and went on anyway. He sat in a wheelchair and the Fool pushed him around the stage. It was wonderful.

GAMBON: What a good idea! If Lear came on at the beginning of the play, pushed in a wheelchair by the Fool, he plays infirm, he pretends to be old and doddery. To excuse himself from the rigours of the kingdom and all that, he divides his kingdom. That's a brilliant idea. And then when Cordelia says no, up he gets. The audience would think, 'By Christ!' And he retreats back to the wheelchair and then finally they cast him out into the storm and he hurtles across the stage in the wheelchair and is pushed out the doors of the castle. If you mention that to Adrian Noble, he'd do it.

MG: He'd ask you to do it again. Or maybe he'd ask Antony Sher, as a follow-up to his Richard III on crutches.

GAMBON: I'll ring him up and tell him. No, a wheelchair wouldn't be physical enough for Tony. Tony'll play him on a motorbike.

MG: At the National, McKellen is doing Richard III and Brian Cox is playing Lear.

GAMBON: Double them up. It's like a big sausage machine, Lears and Richard IIIs coming out on an endless conveyor belt.

MG: After you take time to do Maigret on television, they'll plead with you to come back to the stage.

GAMBON: They'd give me a car then.

MG: And a parking space. There's always that temptation to stay in films and television. If Olivier's career in films had gone better, he might have moved to Hollywood.

GAMBON: I don't know. Olivier was such a consummate theatre man.

MG: Do you take a role offstage with you?

GAMBON: Yes, they do stick with me. This one [in *Man of the Moment*] hasn't affected me much, because he's such an ordinary man. He's not depressed. Eddie [Carbone] took me over. King Lear certainly took me over. Well, I was walking around with a great big white beard, my own beard. You can't help but be Lear when you look like that.

MG: But you don't have to act like that when you're offstage.

GAMBON: When you wake up in the morning, and you've got *King Lear* that night, the whole day is destroyed, because you know you've got to go and do that. I don't know what Othello will do to me.

MG: Do you fire those antique guns that you recondition?

GAMBON: No. I can't bear killing animals. Most people who collect antique guns would never dream of using them. They only collect them as some people might collect stamps or Chippendale chairs. They collect them as objects for their shape and form and decoration. The mechanism of firearms attracts me as well. I also like clocks. I work on clocks. Actually collecting clocks and collecting guns go together.

MG: Do you collect cars?

GAMBON: I love cars. I don't collect them.

MG: Can you fix a car?

GAMBON: Yes I can. I've done quite major things on cars. I've had engines out and put in new gear boxes. Except the older you get, the less you want to get your hands dirty, to take the skin off your knuckles lying under a car.

MG: How do you feel about computers?

GAMBON: I don't like them. I don't know anything about them. I'm frightened of them. You can't see how they work. If you open a car up or open the back of a clock you can see exactly how it works. Your eyes will just tell you by following the gears as they revolve. But with a computer . . . They're very powerful tools, aren't they? I got very depressed a few months ago. I wanted some steel plates cut up for my engraving. It's such hard work. I went to this small factory and said, 'Could you make these plates for me?' The man said yes and he showed me round. They were doing things now with computers that we used to do by hand, all those years ago. It's completely revolutionised engineering. These machines are being operated by computers which are programmed. They work to a millionth of an inch. I think that's sad because it takes it away from people. The sort of technology that I know is probably being practised in India and China. An old-fashioned technology.

MG: And real clocks and watches, not the digital kind. Do you wear a watch?

GAMBON [*holding out his wrist*]: Yes, that's a real one. I wouldn't like a watch that you didn't have to wind. I tried to buy some equipment the other day from another firm, and he said that he sent all this stuff to Taiwan. The English don't buy it because they're into computers. Lots of old English machine tools are sent to India and places like that. It's even happening now with cars. I read the other day that in ten years' time, it won't be possible to repair your car on the street because cars would be so technologically advanced. The English gun trade is the last bastion of craftsmanship, where things are made by hand. People make English sporting guns by hand, and they charge £25,000 for one, and there is a four-year waiting list. You can buy the same thing down the road for £200, but it won't last five generations and appreciate in value. I know a lot of people who work in that trade. It's one of my obsessions.

51

MG: What do you talk about with other gun collectors? Guns? Not acting.

GAMBON: Gun collectors tend not to be interested in acting. They don't know much about it. I had an old gun mate who saw the play the other night. It was interesting when he came round afterwards. He knows me at his place, but he didn't know me in here and in what he'd seen on the stage. I could see he was very confused in the dressing room. Didn't know what to say. He was all right when we got out of the building. I suppose it is rather odd. It's an odd job, isn't it?

MG: Egotism is part of it, but there has to be something else.

GAMBON: I think it's creativity, as well – the need to act. You're born with that. It's not just a craft. It's something more than that. I think an actor can add to a writer's work, but you have to be very careful saying that. I sometimes think the public sees so much television that they confuse acting with behaviour. A lot of stuff in soap operas is just behavioural activity, whereas the acting that you do onstage or in good films isn't that at all.

MG: What's the difference?

GAMBON: TV has made acting more commonplace. There are good actors, but the material is poor. They sit back, take it easy and just turn it out.

MG: Has Larry Dalzell always been your agent?

GAMBON: Ever since 1967. Sometimes I'm quite stubborn and I've caused him trouble. I get moods, and he has to cope with it. There's a bit of a prima donna in me – that just dawned on me. I was playing Oscar Wilde in a three-part television adaptation about his life. We were shooting a scene down in Bristol. They wrapped about four o'clock and we were supposed to go to Oxford. I was not happy with the scripts, so I was in a state anyway. We went back to the hotel. I was still dressed as Oscar Wilde – full make-up, big black wig and Edwardian clothes, boots, silk cravat, a silver-tipped cane. I got back to the hotel and my room had been let and my civilian clothes had been lost. So I threw a moody. I ran through the streets of Bristol dressed as Oscar Wilde with the production manager chasing after me in his car. I managed to get away from him by leaping over the central barrier of a motorway that runs through the middle of Bristol. I crossed the motorway as Oscar Wilde, went into the main station and bought a first-class ticket to London.

MG: Still as Oscar Wilde?

GAMBON: Yeah, oh yeah. And all the while shouting obscenities at this man whenever he caught up with me. I got into the train and went to London as Oscar Wilde. I was dying with unhappiness. I went into the buffet car and got completely pissed. When I got to Paddington Station, the BBC big boys were at the barrier, waiting. The anger had died in the train, but when I got to the barrier, I managed to get it back up again, and I threatened to kill them. I handed the inspector the ticket, and I ran, and they ran after me. I jumped into a cab and went home. And by that time I was deep in the shit. You know you do these terrible things, and they get worse and worse, and you regret it, but you won't give in. We were supposed to be in Oxford for the following day's shooting. They sent a car at five in the morning to pick me and take me to Oxford. And they never referred to it when I got there. They pretended: 'Good morning, Michael.' So I am temperamental.

MG: You're also known as a practical joker.

GAMBON: I think that's been exaggerated. I don't fool around more than any other actors. Peter Bowles is just as bad. It's boredom that causes that, the repeatability of being in plays. Stephen Moore and I are very bad together. We used to carry water pistols in the plays we were in at the National. We always had water pistols, fully loaded. In *Othello*, *Sisterly Feelings*.

MG: I don't remember any water pistols in *Othello* or *Sisterly Feelings*.

GAMBON: Oh, you wouldn't have seen it. [*Laughter.*] We'd have them in pockets, hidden. And as soon as the blackouts come, you let them have it. Silly, childish. I got so bad that in my workshop I started to develop a water pistol that would be the best water pistol that's ever been. I've never come across a good one. They're always plastic shit, or they're made for children, or they're rubbish. I went through a whole thing of thinking that all these yuppies with lots of money would just love to have a water pistol which they'd wear in their suit. They could use it at a dinner party or in the office or on the underground. It could be beautifully made. I could charge a fortune for it. I'd actually started to do some drawings. It's a very difficult thing to design, because obviously it mustn't leak. So I was going to make it engraved and inlay it with mother of pearl, make them beautiful things, and probably get an outlet through Harrods. But it all fell through; it was just daydreaming.

MG: In *Sisterly Feelings*, you tossed a coin to determine the course of the play. You made a two-headed, or two-tailed coin and used that instead.

GAMBON: Oh, yes. The play was split into two principal sections and within each of those two there were two other variants. It genuinely worked on the toss of the coin as to which way we did it. In my machine shop I cut the coin in half and then cut another one in half, and brazed them together. Polished them up so you couldn't tell, the line was so fine. I gave the coin to Steve Moore who was the guy with the coin in the play, and we used that most nights, apart from when we felt we were going to get into trouble.

MG: Did Ayckbourn know?

GAMBON: Well, I think it backfired on us, because when the production closed, we sent the coin to Alan with a little note. We never got a reply. He never mentioned it.

MG: I think he was the one who told me about it. My interpretation of the story is that you and Moore wanted to play your own way.

GAMBON: We didn't do too well if it came out heads. If it came out tails, it meant I had half the play off, and he had an easier time too. I made the coin tails because if it was heads, it meant we had to do more.

MG: If the other actors found out . . .

GAMBON: They wouldn't have liked it. The idea was to get off, not to stay on. Because in a long run, you get a bit cheesed off.

MG: In Ayckbourn's *Intimate Exchanges*, everything turns on whether or not the woman lights up a cigarette in the first scene. There are 18 if not 36 variations.

GAMBON: It wouldn't be worthwhile fixing that play, would it? Michael Bryant got a bit bored in *Sisterly Feelings* and put on a funny voice. He found himself trapped with this voice that didn't belong to him, and having started the play he could not stop. Have I said anything of interest today, Mel?

MG: Yes, I learned about cars and . . .

GAMBON: Water pistols.

'The tradition of acting is based on copying. It's passed on from one actor to another'

In the afternoon, I met Gambon at the National Theatre. We each had three cups of coffee as we talked about Olivier, The Singing Detective *and other matters.*

MG: In the book *Olivier at Work*, you and 35 other actors, playwrights and directors talk about working with him. You recalled, as a junior member of the Old Vic company on tour in Birmingham, you had coffee with him and a few other actors. You said, 'walking along the street with the greatest actor in the world,' you were annoyed that no-one recognised him. There was, you said, 'no reflected glory.'

GAMBON: I was very disappointed. It was nice to be with someone as famous as that, to be seen with him, but no-one recognised him. Olivier looked a bit like a bank manager when he was off the stage, if he wanted to. He'd wear a trilby hat and a coat, and no-one would give him a second look. He wasn't a particularly tall man.

MG: Once after I interviewed him in New York, we left his hotel and went to a movie theatre where he was meeting Garson Kanin and Ruth Gordon. They were not there yet. There was a long line at the movie, and I asked him if he wanted me to wait with him until they came. He said no and he stood in line. As I walked away, I looked around and not a soul recognised him – and there was a line all the way down the street. I wasn't sure if he didn't want to be recognised or if simply he looked too nondescript to be noticed.

GAMBON: I think he switched off, if he chose to.

MG: Have there been actors wanting to bask in your reflected glory?

GAMBON: No, I don't think so. I hadn't thought of it like that. I thought they just wanted to be my friends.

MG: In that piece about Olivier, you mentioned the copper band he wore on his wrist, and that other actors started to wear copper bands. Do you wear a copper band?

GAMBON: No, I don't, but a lot of us did then. That was to stop rheumatism. But I noticed quite a few copper bands went on after he started wearing one. We were just in awe of him. Well, he was the most famous actor in the world, wasn't he? And being with him every day was like a privilege, a joy. We all felt that were very lucky.

MG: Would you mimic him?

GAMBON: I think a lot of acting, the tradition of acting is based on copying. It's passed on from one actor to another. For instance, Tony Hopkins's acting is greatly influenced by Olivier. Vocally, mainly, I think. I think all actors are. They hear, they copy things. They hear Olivier, and the same with Richardson or Scofield – they're just little tools to help you. I think it's quite healthy to copy people.

MG: Could you specify how you may been influenced by other actors?

GAMBON: When we did *A View from the Bridge*, the whole company was rather reluctant about doing the Brooklyn accent. So we studied tapes. The only tapes that are readily available of Brooklyn accents are the whole range of that New York Italian accent that appears in *The Godfather*, *Mean Streets*, which is one of my favourite films, *Taxi Driver*,

Raging Bull. So we listened to those endlessly, recordings of the soundtracks, and learned a lot from them in terms of vocal rhythms . . . That's not quite the same thing.

MG: It isn't the same as being part of the English acting tradition. It isn't just the symbols, it's the actual . . .

GAMBON: Techniques. Using Olivier's vocal techniques sometimes helps in the formation of speeches in Shakespeare, that clipped delivery. [*His speech is clipped as he talks about it.*] And the bringing the line up at the end, as he used to do. By clipping the words, it makes the speeches easier to control, makes the breathing easier. So if you listen to Olivier and keep that in mind, he just influences you. You can see why he did what he did.

MG: Would you watch Olivier's Othello before you did the play?

GAMBON: I hadn't thought of that, but I probably would have done it anyway, if you hadn't mentioned it. I was in the film, just a non-speaking part. Yes, I will watch bits.

MG: You'll fast-forward to your part?

GAMBON: Yes, yes. [*Laughter.*] I don't think there's anything wrong with watching a video of how someone else did it. It might solve a few problems.

MG: You were with the Old Vic from 1963 to 1967?

GAMBON: About three-and-a-half years.

MG: That would have been very important because you were young and untrained.

GAMBON: And inexperienced.

MG: In the Olivier book, it lists the casts on those plays. There were four in which you were named. One was Peter O'Toole's *Hamlet*, and it didn't say which part you played.

GAMBON: I was a spear-carrier.

MG: You were a servant in *The Recruiting Officer*, a character named Snap in *Love for Love* and Jerry Devine in *Juno and the Paycock*.

GAMBON: That was a good part. I was also Eilif in *Mother Courage*. They were two good supporting parts, Jerry Devine and Eilif. And I played a small featured part, Diego de Trajillo, in *The Royal Hunt of the Sun*. It wasn't that I'd spent the three-and-a-half years doing nothing. The parts got slightly bigger.

MG: It was good experience, just being there?

GAMBON: Yes, except towards the end. I got a bit frustrated. If you're an actor, you always want to play the leading part. I think that's human nature. I wanted to do more, so that's why I left.

MG: Was it difficult for you to confront Olivier?

GAMBON: No, he was very approachable. He made it quite clear to the actors that his time was theirs. You could approach him about anything professional any time you wanted to. At the end of a year's contract, we had to go and see him to stay on for another year. He gave me some advice. He said, 'We want you to stay on for another year, but I might add that I want you to have voice classes.' We had a full-time teacher there, and my name wasn't very often on the list. You were supposed to turn up, but I never used to turn up. So Olivier gave me that sort of bollocking. The next year I went to the classes.

MG: As you said before, you're largely untrained. That might qualify you for playing Ayckbourn but you're also a Shakespearean actor. Where does your voice come from?

GAMBON: I think it's to do with the way you're physically born. My chest, from the sternum to the spine, is as deep as it is here, so it's shaped like a barrel. It's dead round. I think that helps; to be shaped like that is better for classical acting, because it gives your voice a certain tone.

MG: But Gielgud and McKellen aren't shaped that way.

GAMBON: Fucks that theory. Well, I don't know. Paul Scofield is.

MG: And Albert Finney is a short barrel.

GAMBON: Oh, Albert's the same, and Simon Callow. That's all bullshit maybe. I don't know. They're all, or have been, smokers. I think that helps. I think it makes the voice. Certainly Olivier smoked quite heavily. And Gielgud always had a fag in his mouth. Alan Howard is a chimney. Ron Pickup, my dear friend Ron Pickup, he *is* a cigarette.

MG: First, you have to have a barrel chest, then you have to smoke. What about drinking? Does that help give you resonance?

GAMBON: I don't know if that makes a difference. Anything helps.

MG: Richard Burton might be next to Olivier, in terms of having a full voice.

GAMBON: He had a barrel chest, and he was a smoker. If he wasn't, he should have been.

MG: And a drinker.

GAMBON: And a drinker. My theory is not unfounded.

MG: Does that mean if you weren't built as you are, you might not have been the actor that you are?

GAMBON: I'd have probably been a lighter actor. I would have been more ethereal.

MG: *More* ethereal?

GAMBON: I would have been an ethereal actor.

MG: You wouldn't prefer to be an ethereal actor?

GAMBON: No, but I'd like to be a bit ethereal. Well, I am a bit ethereal.

MG: Well, you are light on your feet.

GAMBON: Yes, but those guys who can play Mercutio, I envy them to have that facility with the text, the Queen Mab speech. I've never been much good at that sort of thing, Restoration-type acting, Witwoud in *The Way of the World*.

MG: That production of *Much Ado* at the National was not a happy one.

GAMBON: I wasn't any good. I just didn't enjoy it.

MG: But with that quick wit and repartee.

GAMBON: That didn't sit on me very easily. Maybe I'm a slow-pace actor. I couldn't get on top of *Much Ado*. We were also acting on a carpet, which didn't help.

MG: You prefer bare floors?

GAMBON: No, it's something to do with shoes again. It's very wrong to play *Much Ado* on a carpet that doesn't make a noise when you walk. It's the wrong sensation. It would be all right if you were in a Simon Gray play, in a living room. There would be a carpet.

MG: But in *Lear* and *Antony and Cleopatra*.

GAMBON: There would be no carpets there. You couldn't do those on a carpet, because you can't hear the feet.

MG: Boots on a bare floor.

GAMBON: Boots on a bare floor are great. It's something to do with the noise.

MG: Peter Brook is a great believer in carpets. He uses them whenever he can fit them in.

GAMBON: And some people do sand. They act on sand, in sand pits. Wasn't there a production of *Troilus and Cressida* in a sand pit?

MG: McKellen did *Coriolanus* in a sand pit. Irene Worth sat in the sand with her parasol.

GAMBON: I don't see how you can act in a sand pit. Sand would be the worst. Carpets would be second.

MG: *Sisterly Feelings* was on earth.

GAMBON: That was supposed to be on grass.

MG: A grassy knoll.

GAMBON: A grassy knoll, that's all right.

MG: It never bothers you if a character is villainous?

GAMBON: No. What Robert De Niro did in *Raging Bull* was the most remarkable achievement, because there is not one frame in the film where he wants you to feel sorry for him.

MG: Would you set any parameters about playing an unsympathetic character?

GAMBON: I wouldn't be in a play that was overtly anti-Semitic or written by a fascist bastard. I think a lot of actors tend to twist and turn plays and texts to make the character they play loved. It doesn't matter if you like him. But I quite like old King Lear. He's mad at the beginning and he does crazy things, but in the end he comes around and you see the real man. He wakes up and sees all his wrongs. He's stripped bare. At the end you see the real man with the dead child. He comes full circle and sees the evil around him. Galileo is just a worker for what he saw as the truth – in Brecht's version – and scientific knowledge. At the same time, he warns against how clever we will become, that one day we will kill ourselves, which looks like it's coming true.

MG: How did you come to do *The Singing Detective*?

GAMBON: It just came to me. You can see how vast it is, six episodes, eight hours. It was complicated stuff. But I read it and I had to play it. I thought it was a masterpiece. Met the director [Jon Amiel], had a chat and we started. It was helped by the fact that we did it in two sections, where the man was in bed in hospital. We did that in three months. And then we did all the stuff of the Singing Detective: the trenchcoat and the mac, the cigarette, the crooning, the lipsynch and all the fantasy. It was like two complete blocks of film, separated pretty well down the middle.

MG: How much of your characterisation was based on Dennis Potter himself?

GAMBON: I met him just a few times, and he came to a few rehearsals. I watched how he held a cup. [*He demonstrates.*] He had psoriatic arthropathy – that means that the knee joints, the ankle joints, thigh, top of the spine, the hands slowly fold in and get locked in that position. I watched him doing that and how he held a cigarette. That's all really, because everything he wrote – the man in the hospital – is there in the script. There's not much to research. You have to keep one step ahead of the script. It's like having a flow chart in your brain, a flow chart of emotions so that there is plenty of light and shade. You can't relax and you certainly can't walk it. It was taxing on the brain.

MG: Was it difficult for you to remain immobilised?

GAMBON: No. It was a very good experience to suddenly find yourself having to play for three months in a bed, and not be able to move.

MG: And in the other half of the character, you do move.

GAMBON: He has this sort of rolling gait. His hands were always like that in all the filming we did in the hospital. His hands were buckled with heavy makeup. I used to double-joint my thumb: it looked hideous. And I put everything I had – call it angst – into that, whether it was underneath the sheets or on top of the sheets.

MG: When you weren't performing, did you find yourself being more physical, working out – in order to compensate?

GAMBON: No. It was just so bloody tiring doing it. By the end of a day's shooting, we were dead. But also that psoriasis make-up, it's very delicate, so you could only shoot close-ups

63

in the morning, because it would just fall off. We always did close-ups and intense scenes early in the morning.

MG: Did you ever lose your temper?

GAMBON: Yes I did, but only inasmuch as you're under stress in those situations. I remember shouting once when he kept me sitting there all day and didn't use me. He had me in all the bloody stuff, bandages, and I blew up, but I apologised.

MG: Did you do your own singing?

GAMBON: No, that was all lipsynch. For three months I walked around with a Walkman and a headset, listening over and over. The timing had to be perfect. Because it was so disjointed, such a complex script, the director said to me one day when we were filming, 'What do you think of it?' I said I thought it was good, what do you think? He said, 'I think it's good, but I can't tell.' Then when it was all cut together, there was a showing at BAFTA, and it was extraordinary. We knew we had a hit. Afterwards there were great crowds of people around us, interviewing us, I couldn't believe it. And then the night it didn't win the award at the BAFTA show was terrible. It lost to *The Lives and Loves of a She-Devil* – a TV adaptation of a novel which shouldn't be in that category: Best Series. How can you put a television adaptation of a novel up against the original writing of Dennis Potter? When it didn't get Best Series, there was a gasp – 2000 people. [*He gasps in memory.*] They couldn't believe it. I got one for the actor, but there was a hush. It was obviously a deliberate plan to smack Dennis Potter in the face. They just didn't like him. It was too intelligent for them.

MG: Do you have any interest in directing? I noticed that you directed a platform performance at the National.

GAMBON: A play by Richard Harris, the comedy writer not the actor. It was just on at six o'clock for an hour, with three actors: Diana Bull, Russell Dickson and Marcia Warren. I didn't direct them. I just sat there. There wasn't a lot of movement. It was set in a hospital, a man in a bed and two women, at each side of the bed. The main thing to do was to arrange when the curtain went up and when the lights came up. I didn't enjoy it. I didn't know what to say to them. I felt rather guilty. I thought, this isn't what a director should do. Occasionally I would say, 'Don't do that.' I was very embarrassed. I said, 'If you take your handkerchief out of your handbag now, they won't listen to what he's saying.'

MG: That sounds like good direction.

GAMBON: That's sort of an actor's direction. Directors don't normally say that sort of thing. I said that because the play isn't about the handkerchief. It's about what he says. That's like a child directing.

MG: Or like an actor. A number of directors have been actors. That can be an asset.

GAMBON: Oh, yes. They watch your back for you.

MG: But you have no interest in directing?

GAMBON: The only interest I have is that many of them in the West End sit at home every night while we work our backs off, and they collect big cheques every Friday. For doing nothing. So I would like to [*pause*] be a director. [*Loud laughter.*]

MG: Did you ever meet Peggy Ramsay, the play agent?

GAMBON: You know I was in [her client] Chris Hampton's *Tales from Hollywood.* I met her at a do at the Savoy Hotel. She was talking to me and she said, 'Christopher wrote a wonderful play, *Tales from Hollywood.* Destroyed by that idiot who played the leading role. It was just shocking. Why did they ever give it to him?'

MG: Did you tell her that you were that actor?

GAMBON: Oh, god no. I daren't.

'So I ran over and killed the rabbit'

We were due to meet at the stage door at the National at noon. As usual, Gambon was a bit early. Over coffee, he expressed an interest in my tape recorder and my growing collection of tapes of us talking. Later we went upstairs to the Lyttelton buffet and had lunch, and still later we drove to a suburb of London to see a gunmaker that he knew.

GAMBON: You could play these tapes late at night when you can't sleep. That's what Dennis Potter said at one of the rehearsals of *The Singing Detective*. He can be very cruel. Two old actors were sitting there talking about their experiences in rep and he was sitting opposite them. At the end of their long conversation, he said, 'You know, I wish I'd recorded that conversation between the two of you because then I could have played it late at night when I couldn't sleep.' That's a very Dennis Potter remark.

MG: You've had a long working relationship with Pinter.

GAMBON: I did *Betrayal*, *Mountain Language*, *The Heat of the Day*, *Turtle Diary* – and *Old Times* on the West End with Liv Ullmann.

MG: You replaced Pinter in *Veterans' Day* and he replaced you in *Old Times*. What do you think of him as an actor?

GAMBON: I think he's terrific. Did you see him on television in *The Birthday Party*? He played Goldberg, with a moustache. Wonderful, evil – he looks totally different with a moustache. He looks like a real hood, whereas without the moustache, he looks like a writer, doesn't he? I just acted with him last week. We did *Betrayal* on the radio. Two days' work. He was superb. He said, 'I wouldn't fancy doing this all the time, this acting business.'

MG: Starting with *Otherwise Engaged* [which Pinter directed], he bears a responsibility for your career.

GAMBON: I owe a great deal to him. He's a good director. Very straightforward. His directing is like his writing, pared to the bone.

MG: You like to work with directors who have been actors?

GAMBON: Yes, at least they know what it's like. Peter Gill was an actor, too, and he's a wonderful director. You learn so much about acting in the rehearsal room because he has a terrific ear. I've watched him make actors say lines like they've never been said before. He taught me to give real value to the words. I heard Natasha Richardson talking about acting on the radio yesterday, and she said, she doesn't want to keep churning it out because it goes stale. And it worried me because maybe that's what I do. I go from one to the other and it just keeps churning, churning, churning. Then again I thought, she's wrong because if it's your job, then that's what you do.

MG: In describing your performances, people have occasionally compared you to animals, to bears, gorillas and lions. One review said you were like a giant sea anemone.

GAMBON: Oh, shit! Really?

MG: I guess he meant sort of like an octopus.

GAMBON: Long arms, and a bent back, sort of round, stooped back.

MG: Do you think in animal images?

GAMBON: One of the exercises at Stratford with Adrian Noble: we pretended to be animals. When we were doing *Antony and Cleopatra*, it was just me and Helen Mirren in the big room. He said, 'I want you, Helen, to be a rabbit, and you, Michael, to be a lion,' and he said [*snaps his fingers*], 'Now!' And so I became a lion. I remember this was terribly funny, and he added quickly, 'There is a steel grill that has come down the centre of the rehearsal room, and there are bars running from me to the wall.' So I went to the bars and looked at the rabbit: she was hopping. I was padding up and down. I started off making a few noises [*a low growl*] and she was going 'Heh, heh, heh' [*panting*]. Rabbits don't make a noise. After 10 minutes of doing that, you get a bit embarrassed. After about 15 minutes, the mind clicks off and you say, 'Oh, fuck this.' The bastard is sitting there smoking [*he imitates Noble sitting back looking smug*], saying nothing and watching these two actors who by that time are well out of character. So I went and curled up in a corner and she curled up, and that was it. It must have been an hour, and then in a loud voice, he said, 'The steel grill is now being lifted up.' I thought, oh shit, and then he said, 'The steel grill is gone, there is nothing between the two of you.' So I ran over and killed the rabbit!

One day he had Helen put her hand on the floor, and I put my hand opposite, and then we studied each other's hands for half an hour, staring at them, making comparisons. I think it's a way of breaking down barriers between people, or what they [directors] imagine is a way of breaking down barriers between actors. I think they're all tried and tested techniques.

MG: Did you learn anything from that hand exercise?

GAMBON: I realised she had very bad fingernails.

MG: And she realised you have long hands.

GAMBON: Tony [Sher] and I did animal exercises as the Fool and Lear. We did monkeys and all that.

MG: Not all directors do that.

GAMBON: Oh, no. Alan Ayckbourn doesn't. He gets hysterical with laughter if you tell him those stories.

MG: Why don't you like to talk about your life offstage?

GAMBON: I've always compartmentalised my life, totally. I've never mixed the two.

MG: Could you tell me about your growing up?

GAMBON: Well, you know I was born in Ireland. I have a few memories of being a kid. I was born in 1940, and my dad was over here during the war. He was a war reserve policeman in London. He tried to join up, but he didn't pass the medical, so he joined the police. He spent the five years of the war in London while my mother stayed in Dublin. Then in 1945 they brought me over here the day the war ended. I was 5, and I remember being stood on top of a car and looking at the fireworks. I remember the bomb-sites, rows of houses gone.

MG: What memories do you have of Dublin?

GAMBON: I remember seeing funerals with horses with plumes, like in James Joyce. That was a very powerful image. My mother came over to London and didn't know a soul. We went to Camden Town, which was the Irish community in North London, and we lived in a flat. I think she was very lonely and was very much lost in London, with a small child. My mum and dad used to take me back to Ireland every year because my mother missed it terribly. And so I have memories of holidays in Ireland. And then memories of Camden Town between the age of 5 and 13 or 14, principally of being an altar boy in the church up there, St. Aloysius, by which time my brother and sister were born. Then the firm my dad worked for moved, and we moved down to Crayford, which is about 15 miles to the south-east in North Kent. When I was 13, I was a Sea Cadet. That's like a junior branch of the Navy, same uniform as the Royal Navy. I was in in the First City of London Sea Cadet Corps, the St. Clement Dane's unit. On the day of the Coronation in 1953, we were in full kit, gaiters, rifles, bayonets. I loved the uniform.

MG: Did you still feel your roots were in Ireland?

GAMBON: No, my roots were in North London. I used to play in the street in Camden Town, just in front of the Unity Theatre, and it wasn't many years later that I started coming back to that part of London to act there. It was just around the corner from where we lived.

MG: Did you play the banjo?

GAMBON: When I was a kid. I used to go to jazz clubs and try to stand in. I stood in once with a band called Big Bill Brunskill and his Downtown Stompers. They started 'The World is Waiting for the Sunrise.' I was terrible. I knew four chords, and I was playing out of tune.

MG: That was the end of your banjo career?

GAMBON: I played a bit of classical guitar, but I've lost the knack. Oliver Cotton got me on to it years ago. He used to go to a Russian guitar teacher in Fulham, and I started going to him. I made a bit of progress. If someone asked me to play a guitar in a play, I could do it.

MG: Did you have a happy childhood?

GAMBON: I think so. I hardly had a childhood. It was over so quickly. I left school when I was 15, which to my mind, is shocking.

MG: Do you read a lot?

GAMBON: No, I don't. That's not a good admission, is it? But it's true. I don't even read plays unless someone asks me to be in one.

MG: You didn't sit down and read all of Shakespeare?

GAMBON: No. I don't know what happens in *Titus Andronicus*, because I've never read it or seen it. But I know he puts babies in a pie. Doesn't he?

MG: And he cuts off his hand.

GAMBON: He cuts off his hand?

MG: One of our foremost Shakespearean actors . . .

GAMBON: Well, no, I'm not. I haven't done much Shakespeare, have I?

MG: *Lear, Antony and Cleopatra, Much Ado About Nothing.*

GAMBON: And *Othello* in repertory.

MG: From your point of view, McKellen's a Shakespearean actor.

GAMBON: Oh, he's a Shakespearean actor. And Helen's a Shakespearean actor. They've done tens of those leading parts. They really are versed in it.

MG: Now that you're turning 50 you might consider playing Lear again. And what about Richard III?

GAMBON: Oh, no. He says too much. I always feel when I see *Richard III* that he never stops talking. That's why Pinter is so good. None of his people say too much. You've got that wonderful deep subtext. What he says on the top is just like the milk in the tea, the cream in the coffee; it just floats.

MG: The father in *The Homecoming* would be a role for you.

GAMBON: Yes, that's a good part, a comedy part. In the opening scene, the father's talking and Lenny is sitting there reading a newspaper and he looks up and says, 'Why don't you shut up, you daft prat?' When I saw that, I just died with laughter. And the father turns around and says, 'Don't you speak to me like that. I'll chop your spine off, you talk to me like that!'

MG: How do you feel about Shaw?

GAMBON: Oh, I don't like Shaw. I did *Major Barbara* and *The Doctor's Dilemma*. They certainly talk too much, and they are all pompous, aren't they? Know-alls. Great long sweeping sentences.

MG: Perhaps that's one reason you've done so much Pinter and Ayckbourn.

GAMBON: They're quite bare, aren't they? Maybe there's something in that. Maybe that's what attracts me so much.

71

MG: What is the derivation of the name Gambon?

GAMBON: For years, I thought it was French, then I heard some stories from my mother. She said that a Dutchman got someone pregnant in Dublin and ran off and left them. Then I talked to a friend of mine, an Irishman who's a bit of a genealogist. He said Gambon is quite a common name in County Wexford in Ireland. It must be to do with the Spanish Armada, which went aground on the coast along Ireland. I suppose that's why a lot of Irish people are very dark, almost Italian-looking. My dad was dark-looking.

MG: Friends call you Mike?

GAMBON: For the first five or six years, I was always Mike in programmes. I thought it was more 'with-it'. Then I did a series for the BBC and the producer said that Mike was a bit common. So he changed it on the credits and I've kept it ever since.

MG: I suppose the Mike would be part of your informality.

GAMBON: The need to be friendly. I've always wanted to be part of the group in a play, part of the team.

MG: Was that one of your initial reasons for going into the theatre, that you would be part of a group, of a family?

GAMBON: A family, yes. There certainly is a sort of security in the theatre. You walk into a theatre and you're with your colleagues and the little family group, and the outside world is shut out.

MG: The family ends when the show closes.

GAMBON: Very sad. Breaks your heart. You might never see them again. That's a funny thing about being an actor. You become deeply involved with people. And then it's just finished, and you get depressed about it. Both times I've been with Alan Howard in plays and films, I've really missed him terribly at the end. I want to ring him up and yet I don't. You'd think we'd go have a drink, but we don't. Being in a play must be a bit like being in the army in wartime.

MG: You're all united . . .

GAMBON: In adversity, facing the critics.

MG: And the director, possibly.

GAMBON: Maybe the director. Directors must feel quite lonely. Actors tend to get together in a little group and the director sits there alone in the rehearsal room.

After finishing our lunch, he took his car out of the garage. It was raining as we drove to see his gunmaker friend. I asked a few personal questions, which he hesitated to answer.

MG: You were married as a young actor?

GAMBON: Yes.

MG: Was your wife an actress?

GAMBON: No. She's a mathematician. That's an unlikely combination, isn't it?

MG: Are you still married?

GAMBON: That's sort of dodgy. You know what I mean. I think it's enough to say that I'm still married.

MG: And you have a son.

GAMBON: And I have a son.

MG: Is your mother still alive?

GAMBON: Yes she is. She lives out in Crayford, where we moved to when we left London. She just lives on the next street. My brother and sister still live down there, so nothing's changed much, in that respect. I've sort of grown away because of what I do. I get on well with my brother and sister. My mother doesn't really understand what I do.

MG: Is there a family pride in your accomplishments?

GAMBON: From my brother and sister, yes. But I don't think my mother's aware of the theatre. She watches the television.

When I got my medal from the Queen, she didn't know what it was. She's very Irish.

MG: What did the Queen say to you when she gave you your CBE?

GAMBON: As I walked towards her, I heard her say to the man next to her, 'What's it for?' And he said, 'Acting.' She said, 'Oh.' Then she just said, 'What are you in?' I told her and she said, 'Well done.' She put it over my head, and that was it.

MG: Were you ever miscast?

GAMBON: I once did a television version of *French Without Tears*, in which I played a naval commander, very English, and I was totally wrong. I could play it now, but this was over ten years ago, and I couldn't manage it. Bill Gaskill says in his book [*A Sense of Direction: Life at the Royal Court*] that I was miscast as the son in *Mother Courage*. Some actors say there is no such thing as miscasting, but they're wrong. They say that you can play anything. It's not true. I'm certainly happier acting parts where I'm able to get away from me.

MG: What's the closest to you that you've played?

GAMBON: Parts of every part are bits of you. But I don't know who I am. The vet in *The Norman Conquests*, who just walks through and daydreams a lot – I suppose that was quite close to me. I daydream a lot.

While driving and talking, he took a few wrong turns, then found a familiar road. It was 2.20 and the gunsmith's house was not too far away. He started to laugh as he thought about the idea of bringing me to visit this secretive gunsmith in his basement workshop.

MG: How do you feel about gun control?

GAMBON: I approve of that, yes. It's ludicrous, people walking around with guns. There was a man called Mike Ryan, who was a gun freak and belonged to gun clubs and he went out with an automatic rifle and a revolver and wandered through the streets of an English country town [Hungerford] and killed 13 people. It had such an impact in this country that they changed the laws regulating guns. It's much tougher now. They come down on you like a ton of bricks. They insist that anyone that owns any sort of gun has to have steel security cabinets, and you're not allowed to have ammunition in your house.

I've always liked guns as works of art, as antiques. I was collecting guns when I was 12 years old. My dad used to bring them home from junk shops. You could buy them for next to nothing. He'd wander around these old markets in North London and bring them home on Saturday morning, guns and swords and rusty old bits, and we'd hang them on my bedroom wall.

MG: In some circumstances, that might lead to an interest in military history. With you, it's antiques.

GAMBON: It's the craftmanship, the form and line. I collect guns the way some people collect stamps. Sort of a magpie.

MG: How large a collection do you have?

GAMBON: Oh, 250.

MG: That's an arsenal.

GAMBON: But they're all 18th-century. They're so expensive now, they really are a rich man's hobby. It costs thousands. America is the place where collecting antique guns is really a big hobby. They have arms conventions. They hire a great hall and all these collectors come from all over the States and display their collections, all laid out on trestle tables. They present each other with prizes, which is ridiculous. It's like being given a prize for being a rich man.

MG: When you were in New York did you get a chance to go to any gun shops or conventions?

GAMBON: No, I didn't. I never saw New York at all. I was told it was a place to buy big shoes. Here, buying shoes is a problem. One day I had an afternoon off and I passed five shoe stores and couldn't get a pair to fit me.

MG: What size do you wear?

GAMBON: Twelve.

MG: That's a good reason to do a play on Broadway: you can spend more time looking for big shoes.

With that, we arrived at the home of the gunsmith. It was a small, typically suburban house. Gambon opened the boot of his car and took out a large package wrapped in plastic. He carried that and his briefcase to the front door. The gunsmith, wearing a cardigan sweater and looking like a shopkeeper, welcomed him and said, 'I told my daughter-in-law I'm seeing this actor, Michael Gambon. She said, "This actor? He's the best actor on the West End. We've all seen his plays." He led us downstairs to his workshop, a small room jammed with equipment, hundreds of tools, an 18th-century lathe, a gun butt in a vice. The floor was covered in sawdust. He and Gambon talked about their collections. Then Gambon opened his briefcase and took out a pistol and unwrapped the package to reveal another gun. The pistol had carved silver inlay, and the man looked at it admiringly. 'You're an artist,' he said. 'Thank you,' said Gambon, obviously pleased. That exchange was repeated several times. 'I couldn't do that,' said the man. However, he had built his own boat from scratch, not from a kit. Gambon was interested in buying a piece from him to attach to the butt of a gun, but the man said he did not know what to charge. Gambon said he would check Sotheby's for an auction price, but the man discouraged any contact with Sotheby's for reasons of secrecy. That became clear in our subsequent conversation. We went upstairs to have tea, and he showed us some of the things that he had built, including an antique candleholder. He introduced us to his wife. By now, both were fully impressed by their visitor. During the ride back, Gambon spoke again about his interest in guns.

GAMBON: I've developed my own techniques for doing inlay. It's an 18th-century craft. I read books and people would tell me how it was done, but, of course, they were wrong. They were just guessing. Over a long period of time, I worked it out. I'm getting much quicker at it.

MG: Do you paint or make engravings?

GAMBON: I engrave in steel, what they call gun engraving. I've spent several years trying to teach myself, and I'm making pretty good progress. It's allied to the inlay work. It's that form of rococo scroll, that expanding scroll intermixed with shells and floral designs and acanthus leaves. That's where my main interest in firearms lies, in the decoration.

MG: When you finish making a gun, do you fire it?

GAMBON: No. I make antique guns. When I finish one, I don't want anyone to know it's just been made, because then I can't sell it. So really, I'm a faker. I make things that people think are 18th-century. I don't sell them as 18th-century. I let dealers have them, and they pass them on as the real thing. I shouldn't tell you that.

MG: Does it pay well?

GAMBON: The money's irrelevant. I do it because it gives me great satisfaction.

MG: But it's forgery.

GAMBON: Yes, it's absolutely forgery. I was given a real one to restore by a West End dealer, and while I had it in my possession for six months, I took very detailed drawings of it. Then as soon as I finished the job and handed it back to him, I started making a replica.

MG: I'm trying to think of parallels in the theatre.

GAMBON: Well, it's illusion, isn't it? It's pulling the wool over one's eyes.

MG: With guns, you have rules and techniques, so that it can be a perfect copy, but in acting the rules are indefinable.

GAMBON: There aren't any. It's subjective.

MG: Maybe you wish you had gunsmith rules in acting: 'Here's a pattern of how Burbage or Kean played it.'

GAMBON: Maybe not, because I've always played things differently different nights, although what you think is different is often the same to the audience. Little things you do differently take on mammoth proportions in your mind. Even your attitudes change during the run.

MG: These really are individual arts.

GAMBON: One's a craft. Craftmanship is working with your hands, whereas acting is a little bit of art, isn't it?

MG: Tell me about your voice-overs.

GAMBON: I'm the voice of Wisk, washing-up fluid. I'm the washing machine, and I speak.

MG: As a washing machine?

GAMBON: Yes. Hc has a light on the front of his panel, and he lights up. I just speak normally and they put it through a distorting mechanism.

MG: So that it doesn't sound like you?

GAMBON: Oh, people recognise me. My mother knows it's me. She's more impressed by that than she is about going to see the Queen.

MG: Probably the Queen knew you as the voice of Wisk. I won't ask you how you play a washing machine.

GAMBON: I just do it like myself. I do quite a few different products. Sometimes I do three a week. It's amazing, you can earn a lot of money, if you get a really good run.

MG: What else are you the voice of?

GAMBON: Lots of things: Gillette, a deodorant.

MG: Is that different from your washing-up voice?

GAMBON: The most successful voice-over people are the ones who can hide who they are. I'm no good at that. I'm pretty well the same, so consequently I get fewer of them than my colleagues.

MG: It's odd to think of Lear or Galileo doing voice-overs.

GAMBON: Well, they all do it, don't they?

MG [*noticing the ring he is wearing*]: Did you make that large ring?

GAMBON: No. Actors always wear big rings on their little fingers. It's part of the dress of actors. Gielgud always wears a big ring on his little finger. Scofield does. So I thought I would.

MG: The bracelet from Olivier, the ring from Scofield, the pill from Richardson . . .

Is comedy more difficult than tragedy?

GAMBON: I think it is, because you have to get laughs.

MG: Playing tragedy, you want tears.

GAMBON: That's easier. And if you don't get tears, the audience doesn't know. You can't hear the tears.

MG: Have you ever forgotten your lines?

GAMBON: Week before last. I wasn't thinking. It's never very worrying for me, forgetting lines. On several occasions I make them up. It's terrible when you go blank – and you can't think of anything.

MG: The actor's nightmare. As long as you have the presence of mind to do something.

GAMBON: Might happen tonight.

MG: What do you do if the other actor forgets his lines?

GAMBON: You jump in. You go to the rescue.

MG: Was there ever a very long delay while the other actor found his lines?

GAMBON: When I was in *Otherwise Engaged*. I did Alan Bates's second six months with the original actors, but then they left and a takeover cast came in and I stayed with them for six months. The actor who played the drunk journalist dried one night. I couldn't help him, and he just couldn't speak. He went off the stage, went to the prompt corner, asked to look at the script, said he was sorry to the audience and came back onstage through the door.

'I exaggerate every story. I diddle them around the edges, make them much more entertaining and funny'

I met Gambon at Leslie Pyne, Bootmaker, near the Old Vic, where he had gone to have boots and sandal-like shoes made for him for Othello. *When I arrived he was already there, looking at wooden models of his big feet. They looked like boats. The models are made of American maple, and remain on file at Pyne's shop. I suggested that eventually the models of Gambon's big feet will be on exhibition at the Theatre Museum in Covent Garden. Pyne said that having the model of feet on file, someone could call from Alaska and have boots made – as long as his 'feet' were in the shop. He asked Gambon to bring him a drawing of what he wanted, and took out some sample drawings from a drawer, along with a picture of Richard Harris's shoes. Leaving the shop, we drove to the National for tea.*

MG: I had lunch yesterday with Peggy Ramsay and I told her your version of the story about *Tales from Hollywood*. She said that the actor that ruined the play was not you but someone in California. She's a great admirer of yours and has seen everything you've done. Your story is much better. It seems like a classic Peggy story. I also told Peggy that you were a gun collector. She said there were a lot of guns in

David Hare's play *Knuckle*, and she gave him an antique 17th-century gun as an opening night present. It was a beautiful gun, she said, but David hated it because he hates guns. She said, he probably still has it, so tell Michael Gambon to call David Hare and see if he can buy that gun cheaply.

GAMBON: Maybe Peggy Ramsay should buy me a gun for a present. I've done so many plays for her team [Hare, Hampton, Ayckbourn], I must have contributed something to her income. She owes me a gun, I should think.

I've got to take my mother to a funeral tomorrow in St. Albans. Her best friend dropped dead in Dublin last week. They flew the body back. I've got to drive her up there and then wait and come back.

MG: Can't your brother or sister do it?

GAMBON: No, I suppose I'm the only one with free days, at least they think they're free.

MG: In a sense, you don't have a regular job.

GAMBON: In fact, I have a very regular job. You've probably heard this from other actors, being in a play, the day is gone by midday. I get anxious: the afternoons are always a bit tetchy. Not so much with this play, but certainly when I was in *A View from the Bridge*. I wouldn't go anywhere during the day. I used to just lie low. Sometimes I can't even concentrate. I'd just sit and listen to the radio.

MG: Do actors talk a lot about money?

GAMBON: They talk about money all the time. Haven't you noticed that? They're obsessed with it, with the lack of it.

MG: When actors stop talking about money, what do they talk about?

GAMBON: Women. Actresses. They talk about their careers, parts, experiences when they were in rep. There are always lies, of course, gross exaggerations of the truth. But it's lovely hearing actors telling stories that make you laugh. I exaggerate every story, most of them. I enrich them, but that's quite legitimate, isn't it? I diddle them around the edges, make them much more entertaining and funny.

MG: Some more than others?

GAMBON: I always exaggerate the Olivier audition and another true story when I'd just joined the company. I was 23 and I was totally in awe of him. He was just like a god. I'm very rarely late. One day I was an hour early and I was sitting in the canteen in the Old Vic Theatre down in the basement, having a cup of tea, and I was reading a newspaper. I felt someone looking at me, and it was him, and he sat opposite me at the table. Two people in this big canteen. I had my tea and he had his tea. And he was staring at me. I had auditioned for him and I had a walk-on in *Hamlet*, but he didn't know who the fuck I was. He was staring at me through his big dark glasses. And on the table there was a leather wallet, and embossed on it was the word NORGE. I didn't know what to say. I said, 'Norge.' He said, 'What are you talking about?' I said, 'On the wallet.' I remembered when you collect stamps, Norge was on stamps for Norway. I said, 'Someone must have given you that wallet when you played Hamlet at Elsinore.' There was a long pause, and he said, 'Look, I haven't the fucking faintest idea what you're talking about. That is not my wallet and Elsinore isn't in fucking Norway. It's in Denmark, and good morning to you.' He got up and walked away.

I remember when Tony Hopkins and I were sitting next to Olivier in the stalls and he said, 'Where were you born, Tony?' And Tony said, 'Dundee.' Olivier said, 'But I thought you were Welsh.' He said, 'I am.' He said, 'Well, how were you born in Dundee?' He said, 'I wasn't.' He said, 'Where were you born?' He said, 'Bridge End, Wales.' He said, 'But you said Dundee.' Tony said, 'Yes, I know. I didn't mean it.' Olivier said, 'Oh, fuck off.'

MG: Nerves in the presence of greatness?

GAMBON: Yes! Great nerves so you wouldn't know what you were saying.

MG: At that audition for Olivier, you hurt your hand.

GAMBON: I hurt my hand, but I exaggerate that terribly. Sometimes my whole hand is ripped off. Sometimes he calls a nurse. I did hurt my hand. He said, 'Are you all right?' And I said, 'Yes.' It becomes a whole rigmarole.

MG: Did you ever sit down and have a real conversation with Olivier?

GAMBON: No. I found it very difficult to talk to someone one's totally in awe of. When I started doing well in this business, and I met him again years later, I couldn't call him Larry. I never ever addressed him as Larry. John Dexter took me to his country cottage in Sussex, with Joan Plowright, and we were at the dinner table, and I just couldn't call him Larry. He started talking about Leontes in *The Winter's Tale*, about the line, 'There's a spider in my cup.' He said, 'Do you remember that bit?' 'There's a spider in my goblet,' something like that. I said, 'Oh, yes,' and he wanted me to say something about it, but I couldn't.

MG: You froze?

GAMBON: Tongue-tied.

MG: You didn't feel that way about Ralph Richardson?

GAMBON: No, I felt more relaxed with him. But I used to talk to him about non-acting things. His main obsessions were motorbikes and clocks. I talked a lot about clocks to him.

MG: Is there anybody from the past that you'd have liked to meet?

GAMBON: I'd like to have met people like George Stephenson, who invented the steam locomotive as we know it today. He started in the mines as a miner. He couldn't read or write and yet he went on to become a great engineer and inventor. Stephenson's Rocket. The Rocket steam engine. The first ever. It's an amazing story. Hugh Hudson was going to make a film about it all, with Colin Welland scripting it, but the whole thing fell through.

MG: Would you have played Stephenson?

GAMBON: Yes. I was really excited.

MG: If you could have met Stephenson, what would you have said to him?

GAMBON: I wouldn't have said anything to him. I would just liked to spend a couple of days walking around with him and watching the way he lived his life. I'm rather obsessed with that 19th-century technology, which is linked up with firearms as well.

MG: If there were a time machine, that would be your period?

GAMBON: The 1820's.

MG: What was theatre like then?

GAMBON: I think the 1820's would be the place for me in theatre as well, because that was a time of bombast, and the theatre of Drury Lane and Covent Garden and Macready and Kean and all those people, those massive great actors. Wasn't Macready the first modern actor? They say he invented the pause. That was a theatre expression, a Macready, a pause. He was the first one ever to do a massive speech and then stop halfway through and the audience would go. [*He gasps.*] And he'd hold them, then he'd let them drop. Doing 'a Macready'.

MG: Was there 'a Kean'?

GAMBON: Didn't he terrify the audience? He had that ability to frighten the shit out of them. During the Kean-Macready era, there was an actor murdered on the Strand, stabbed in the alleyway near the Adelphi Theatre. By Irving's time, everything had been Victorianised, had been through the Victorian age of respectability. Irving was the first respectable actor, wasn't he?

MG: You would lean more toward the era of non-respectability?

GAMBON: I would. Yes. I think actors have become commonplace. Television has made them more accessible, more ordinary. They're worried about their mortgages.

MG: Kean and Macready weren't worried about mortgages?

GAMBON: I don't think they gave a fuck about a mortgage. But I suppose they were just as interested in money as we are now.

MG: And billing?

GAMBON: Billing, oh, yes. I'm not interested in billing. I think that's dangerous. It's best to keep your head low with billing.

MG: Duck under the title?

GAMBON: Keep low and then you can't be hit.

MG: Olivier luxuriated in his lordness.

GAMBON: Those days have gone, but there's a bit of lament going on now about the theatre of the '60s and Olivier's National Theatre. People sort of pine for it. But it's gone.

MG: But you have actors like Kenneth Branagh, Antony Sher and Simon Callow who are doing everything.

GAMBON: They're men of extraordinary energy, which I don't possess. I do have commitment, and I work hard, but it's not my whole life.

MG: But you couldn't do without it.

GAMBON: No, I couldn't. Well, if I had to, I would. I'm grateful for having it, but it's not everything to me. So I admire the energy of people like that. I'm prepared to let Tony Sher and Simon Callow and Ken Branagh run my life for me. I would love to work with them. I'm not a natural instigator or leader. I'm much happier to be in the wake.

'It's a charmed bloody career that I've had'

Last week, Gambon was losing his voice and cancelled our talks as well as his performance in Man of the Moment. *During that time I saw Alan Ayckbourn and Harold Pinter, and they spoke about him. At Gambon's invitation, I visited him at home in Forest Hill. He lived on a side street in a large, old rambling house set back on an ill-tended lawn. Inside it was sprawling and fairly cluttered. The house looked lived in. He led me to the kitchen where we sat at the table and had tea. His cat Winnie scurried about. Dvořák's Fourth Symphony (he identified the music) was playing on the radio.*

MG: When I talked to Pinter about you, he told me about the actor Terence Rigby, and his fear of flying.

GAMBON: Oh, that was terrible. I took him up in a Cessna 180, a four-seater. He really had this terrible fear of flying and he took a lot of persuading. I said, 'If you sit next to me in the right-hand seat, I'll do everything very gently, and you can see how a plane works. Maybe you won't be frightened.' We took off from Biggin Hill. It was a gentle climb up. Then I levelled out at 2000 feet. Terry was rigid, but he calmed down a bit. I said, 'If you do this, the nose drops, if you do this, the nose goes up,' and 'This is air-traffic control I'm talking to.' All that bollocks. I was going north to Essex. I was going to take him to Ipswich to have a cup of tea and a sandwich. I got over the Thames and it's like a devil in you that fucks up a play. I just wopped a bit of rudder down, put the stick forward, and we went into a very slow drop – and then I had a heart attack. I did the whole thing [*he demonstrates by gasping for breath*] and collapsed against the side screen. [*He laughs loudly.*] He didn't do what you would think. He didn't do anything. He just sat there. Then I said, 'Just a bit of indigestion.'

MG: He didn't collapse in fear?

GAMBON: No, but he was furious. And if I hadn't been flying the plane, he would have hit me. But he calmed down then, and we landed in Ipswich and had our tea, and he finally smiled.

MG: And it cured his fear of flying?

GAMBON: Nooo. I don't think so. Coming back, I did a lot of bollocks. I came in on the radio and asked to use the DME approach at Biggin Hill, all technical bullshit, not necessary. Terry was deeply impressed.

MG: Does that kind of feeling overcome you often? You just said it was like you were in a play and wanted to fuck it up.

GAMBON: I do that. I don't think I'm the only one. A lot of people are like that. You take risks. At The Other Place in Stratford when we were doing *Antony and Cleopatra* – it's a tiny room – we used to corpse and the audience wouldn't know it. It's just amazing what you can do in the theatre – and people will accept it. Fucking around with the text, and laughing, which is a terrible thing because it builds up in you and you can't control it. I'm very good at keeping it back.

MG: I said to Pinter that he had worked with you in almost every combination. He said he had directed you in plays by other writers, that he had appeared opposite you as an actor, that he had replaced you as an actor.

GAMBON: I've done everything with him. He's really a great bloke, although I've never felt comfortable with him. I never know what he's thinking. But he's very enthusiastic, isn't he? When he praises you, he goes over the top. I like Harold because he doesn't say too much in his plays. There's the line and there's a vast subtext, and I think he's like that as a man. He doesn't say things he doesn't mean. He directs like that. If there's no reason to do something, no-one does it.

MG: I also saw Adrian Noble and he said, 'Have you seen Michael's finger-walks?'

GAMBON [*demonstrates by moving his fingers across the kitchen table*]: That was the start of your career and there [*in the centre of the table*] was the pinnacle of success. And then they'd get lifted up and moved back and dropped to the edge. I used to do various people.

MG: Like Olivier?

GAMBON: Olivier just went boom, boom, boom. Straight strides. [*His fingers march straight across the table.*] And some actors went boom, boom and when they hit a brick wall, they'd step sideways. [*His fingers stumble.*] This was an actress at the National in the '60s, just hanging in the air. [*He hooks his finger to the edge of the table as if clinging for dear life. Then, with the other hand, he flicks the finger off – the end of a cliffhanging career – and the actress falls to her doom.*]

MG: Olivier's walk was different from Richardson's?

GAMBON: They'd be the same. They never had setbacks, did they?

MG: As I remember, Richardson took his knocks.

GAMBON: He was knocked for Macbeth. [*Richardson moves straight ahead, but with a slight comical swagger.*]

MG: What sort of finger-walk does Peter O'Toole have?

GAMBON [*demonstrates: O'Toole marches through the desert, lurches and stumbles, falls on his knuckles, then picks himself up and moves ahead*]: I had forgotten about that. I can only do it when I've had a few drinks in the Dirty Duck [in Stratford]. That brings it out. That was a very butch male company that year, 1982: Pete Postlethwaite, Antony Sher, Malcolm Storry, a real heavyweight bunch of sweaty, effing bastards. It was a pretty grim experience to be a woman in that company.

MG: What is the Michael Gambon finger-walk?

GAMBON: Oh, mine is slow and methodical. A lucky walk. [*His fingers step out with determination, but with a certain casualness, as if out for an evening stroll.*] I'm all right. It's a charmed bloody career that I've had.

MG: Alan Ayckbourn said . . .

GAMBON: Oh, you saw him as well? Oh, fuck.

MG: He expressed great appreciation and admiration, but added that you were slow to get into a role.

GAMBON: I do start slow. I get nervous and it takes weeks to get in. Some are easier than others. I couldn't get into this *Man of the Moment*. I couldn't even learn the lines because I never felt I was right for it. I'm too big. I bruised my vocal cords because I'm trying to make him lighter. I'm trying to make his body small. I'm happier when I'm like that. [*He seems to bulk up and lowers his voice.*] I did take a long time.

MG: I'm going to see *The Heat of the Day* [the TV film of the Elizabeth Bowen novel] tomorrow morning. Harold talked about it, especially about one erotic scene that he liked very much.

GAMBON: A scene with me and Patricia Hodge, which is in the darkness. You just hear voices, you just see their silhouettes. A terrific scene, very well written.

MG: What is your role?

GAMBON: He's a mysterious man called Harrison. It's set in wartime London, and he's really an agent, an MI5 man, and he's tracking down an informer, a spy. And in the process of tracking him down, he falls in love or becomes obsessed with a woman, who is the spy's lover. It's an enigmatic part. I liked it. Chris Morahan directed it and it was adapted by Harold.

The audience knows very little about him or where he comes from. Nor did I.

MG: Harold marvelled at the fact that at the same time you were playing the sergeant in his play, *Mountain Language*, at the National, you were doing *Uncle Vanya* across the river, that you would transform yourself from one to the other. A car would scoot you over after *Mountain Language* and you would do *Vanya*.

GAMBON: I enjoyed that. Fundamentally, I'm a lazy person, so I occasionally fight against that by doing too much. That was an example of really putting myself through the mill, two plays in a night.

MG: Adrian Noble and I talked about your Lear. I said that some people thought the play shifted to the Fool. He said, if that were so, it was your doing, that it was a sign of your 'talent and generosity,' so that it became a play about both of them. You didn't feel you were giving something away by letting the Fool have more prominence?

GAMBON: It's not a question of giving something away. That's how we played the scenes in the rehearsal room. I didn't think in terms of that. Mind you, a lot of actors do. I imagine it's like playing a good game of tennis. The better the player you're opposite, the better you are. I'm being too simplistic, but a play, the meaning of a play, is the principle of the thing, not who's winning.

MG: But you might say that each actor wants to make his own mark. When McKellen plays Richard III, Brian Cox is his Buckingham, and McKellen might feel that Cox stole his thunder.

GAMBON: That would be impossible. Buckingham is a dreadful part.

MG: Although I remember in Olivier's movie of *Richard III*, Richardson made an impression as Buckingham.

GAMBON: It's different in a film. Film is much more controllable. The theatre is more rough and tumble than film. I played Buckingham once. I took over the part at the National Theatre when the actor had to leave. I wasn't even in the show before and they said, will you do Buckingham for the last five performances of John Wood's *Richard III*? I learned it in two days and I went on and did it. John Wood couldn't wait around. He's like a bullet, that guy. If you can't get your line in quick, you don't say it, which I sympathise with a bit. Somehow the leading actor always knows the whole rhythm of the piece. He might seem to be selfish, but he alone can dictate the pace of the evening, and if he's conscious of people slowing down the machine, he'll elbow them out of the way.

MG: Did you feel that way when you were doing Galileo or Lear, captain of the team as well as lead actor?

GAMBON: I certainly did in *Galileo*. I was conscious of the production creaking as we got into the run, and John [Dexter] wasn't there to oversee it. That's very irksome, because you have an overall view of the rhythm and it keeps getting spoiled. Cues come in wrong or stage management teams change, or other actors come in.

MG: How did you feel when Peter Hall asked you to do *Galileo*?

GAMBON: It was a surprise, and I was, as usual, terrified. I didn't know the play. I had never seen it. I had read it. I was delighted. I just said yes, and then I was worried about John, because he had this reputation of being a tyrant. He's not really. I did know one thing, that the production was offered to another director, who turned it down because I had been precast.

MG: I'd heard that originally they were thinking about Albert Finney and Colin Blakely, but then Hall said you were the one.

GAMBON: I didn't know that. I was in the canteen and I got a message, would I go up to his office. And I went up there and he said, 'Do you want to play Galileo?' And he gave me the script. It was as simple as that. I said, 'Yes, thank you.' And it changed my life.

MG: Because people realised that you could do . . .

GAMBON: Classical acting. Big stuff.

MG: We've talked about your early days at the National. You were there when it first started.

GAMBON: On the twenty-fifth anniversary of the National Theatre, the year before last, I was in *Mountain Language*, and I was the only actor who had been there the day it started and was there on that day twenty-five years later. I was very proud.

MG: Ayckbourn feels very strongly that you have a macho image, and that was really important in terms of the roles you've played. That is in contrast to the effete quality that some people associate with English classical acting.

GAMBON: He says I'm quite butch? I also like to do the other bit, though, play the effete. I see myself as being effete.

MG: Effete?

GAMBON: Effete, or a combination of the two. I'd like to be a lyrical actor. Is that what it is?

MG: More Gielgud than Olivier?

GAMBON: Yes, although Olivier could be lyrical. But I love the gentleness. Othello is a good example, because he's very macho. But then he goes into the depths of despair and gets so poetic and savage. That's a touch of lyricism here. It's a good combination. That's what attracts me as well.

MG: When I think of macho actors, I think of Richard Burton, Peter O'Toole, Richard Harris, none of whom really had the full classical career that they were capable of having.

GAMBON: Maybe they got to a certain age and thought they couldn't take any more of this theatre acting. It's a very disciplined, hard life, acting onstage. If you go away, it must be difficult to afford to go back.

MG: Adrian Noble said that one problem was to get an actor to commit himself to a year or a year and a half at Stratford.

GAMBON: Two years. It's committing yourself to being penniless for a long time. For what? For glory? That's OK, but once you've got a bit of glory, you think, I've had enough glory, I want some money.

MG: Are you looking forward to Scarborough?

GAMBON: I've got an apartment there. Get some boiled eggs in and some salad. Live like a monk, play Othello. *Othello* plays for a month, and while that's playing I'll learn *Taking Steps* during the day. That's a real Ayckbourn farce, in which I play a drunk. At the top of the play, he's pissed out of his skull and he gets worse and worse, and in the end he can hardly stand. That suits me fine.

MG: When Olivier played Othello, some people thought he was playing a Jamaican bus driver.

GAMBON: In the wings, he would say, 'No standing on the top deck,' which is what black West Indian conductors used to say in London in the '50s when they they were working on buses. Olivier looked magnificent, which is half the battle.

MG: You said that you didn't think your Benedick worked, and yet it was Peter Gill who directed it. You also said Gill was one of the directors who helped you.

GAMBON: I just felt uncomfortable. I couldn't get into that part. I didn't know how to do it.

MG: Adrian Noble said that when you were at Stratford, you watched Derek Jacobi do Benedick on a TV monitor, and you said, 'Oh, that's how it's done.'

GAMBON: That's true. With Derek, it was like watching him

open the door. I thought, fuck it, that's how to play it. And I also noticed in that production – Terry Hands directed it – everything that I found difficult they cut. I don't mean that critically of Terry Hands and Derek Jacobi: they just made the whole play more accessible. Did Adrian say anything about *Antony*?

MG: He said that you and Helen Mirren had something going together, which added to the play. I asked him about your lion and rabbit story. He said, 'Well, I guess we did some exercises.' I said what did that add up to, and he said it frees actors.

GAMBON: He took us to church once, me and the girl who played Cordelia. There's a speech at the end of *King Lear* when they're arrested and Lear says he'll pray and sing 'and laugh at gilded butterflies.' He had us sitting in a church in Stratford saying the fucking lines. I went along with it. I didn't understand and I don't think he did either.

MG: You tend to go along with directors even when they make odd requests?

GAMBON: You never know. Some door might open. Something might click. Why not do everything?

After tea, he showed me his small, skylit machine shop behind the kitchen. He said that his real machine shop was in another building down the street. The one in his home was crammed with tools and guns in various states of repair, a miniature version of the lair of the gunsmith we visited. Gambon seemed to have something of the same feeling of protectiveness: watch out for burglars! With great pride, he showed me a photograph of a beautifully engraved antique gun that he had created. He said, 'I have boxes of old guns. I get them at Sotheby's and Christie's.' He took out another pistol. 'This is a John Manton gold-inlay duelling pistol. He was one of the great makers of English firearms.' On the wall was a photograph, taken in 1898, of men working in the Holland &

Holland factory. In one corner of the room was a safe, which he said was filled with pistols.

In the hallway were posters from his shows and in the living room various awards (two Oliviers, an Evening Standard, a BAFTA); photographs of his mother and father standing side by side as if in a portrait in a Victorian album; a photograph of Dame Edna with him, Tim Pigott-Smith, David Suchet and Malcolm McDowell when they appeared on her show. A grandfather clock dominated the hallway, part of his collection of timepieces. In another corner there was a collection of microscopes and near its shelves of first editions of books on antiquarian guns. Wherever one turned, there seemed to be a collection. To the rear of the house was a garden-like room, a kind of greenhouse filled with flowers. The house was sunny and cheerful. He did not show me the rest of it, but he said he would like to sell it and move further out into the country.

Mother Courage and Her Children by Bertolt Brecht
Lynn Redgrave (Kattrin), Gambon (Eilif), Madge Ryan (Mother Courage)
and George Innes (Swiss Cheese). National Theatre Company
at the Old Vic Theatre, London, May 1965, directed by William Gaskill
Photo © John Timbers

Betrayal by Harold Pinter
Daniel Massey (Robert), Gambon (Jerry) and Penelope Wilton (Emma).
National Theatre, London, November 1978, directed by Peter Hall
Photo © Michael Mayhew

Galileo by Bertolt Brecht

Gambon (Galileo), James Hayes (Federzoni), Michael Thomas (Sarti as a young boy) and Simon Callow (Fulganzio). National Theatre, London, August 1980, directed by John Dexter.   *Photo © Zoë Dominic*

King Lear by William Shakespeare
Gambon (Lear). Royal Shakespeare Company, Stratford-upon-Avon,
June 1982, directed by Adrian Noble
Photo: Joe Cocks Studio Collection © Shakespeare Birthplace Trust

A View from the Bridge by Arthur Miller
Gambon (Eddie Carbone) in rehearsal.
National Theatre, London, February 1987, directed by Alan Ayckbourn
Photo © Nobby Clark

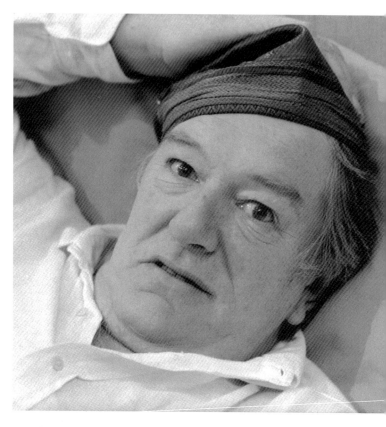

Volpone by Ben Jonson
Gambon (Volpone) in rehearsal. National Theatre, London, July 1995,
directed by Matthew Warchus

Opposite: **A Number** by Caryl Churchill
Gambon (Salter). Royal Court Theatre, London, September 2002,
directed by Stephen Daldry

Photos © Ivan Kyncl

Maigret based on the novels by Georges Simenon
Gambon (Inspector Maigret)
whilst filming the Granada/Mobil Masterpiece
co-production in Budapest, September 1991
Photo © John Timbers

'It's like a compulsion.
I have to do it'

*Still sick, Gambon missed several more performances and can-
celled a meeting with me on Saturday before the five o'clock
matinee. We met on Monday for lunch at the National after he
had been to a memorial for Jim Henson. In the interim I had
seen his actor friends, Oliver Cotton and Stephen Moore, and
he was eager to know what they had said about him.*

MG: They told me a story about the Oscar Wilde film, when
some interviewer asked you why you chose to play the role.

GAMBON: That was a terrible thing I said to that man. I just
couldn't resist it. He said, 'Did you find the part difficult to
play?' I said, 'In what way? How do you mean?' He said,
'Well, the fact that he was a homosexual.' I said, 'No. I used
to be one myself, so I found it very easy.' And as I said it, I
could see him moving around in his seat, and I waited and
then I said, 'But I had to give up being one. It made my eyes
water.'

That was cruel of me. But that was a stupid question. Why
should it be more difficult than playing any other part?
Anyway, you don't play a homosexual, do you? People are
homosexuals, full stop, and then they behave the way anyone
else behaves. It doesn't mean you have to wave your arms
around in the air.

MG: Have you often faced unknowing interviewers?

GAMBON: It's like radio journalists who shove a microphone
in front of you. It's got nothing to do with what you do for a

living. They have no knowledge of acting or of your job. People don't understand about acting. Liking good theatre is a minority taste. You look out there some nights in our theatre and you see the vast majority of men in the audience are asleep, not asleep, but they're not with it. I think they get taken there by their wives.

MG: Somebody once said the only time some men sleep with their wives is in the theatre. What do you do when you see somebody asleep?

GAMBON: You just say, oh, he's asleep. I would worry if it happened in the first three weeks. But now we're used to audiences not being so sharp. I think the audience subtly changes in a long run.

MG: We haven't talked much about actresses, except for Helen Mirren. You and Judi Dench did *Ghosts* on television.

GAMBON: And I've worked with Judi before at the Aldwych. I've worked with a lot of major actresses here. Glenda Jackson. Geraldine McEwan. They're all excellent actresses. Dorothy Tutin. Liv Ullmann. Oh, hundreds.

MG: Who's your favourite?

GAMBON: My favourite's Helen. But that's unfair, isn't it? They're all brilliant.

MG: Some are more brilliant than others.

GAMBON: Chemically, I love Helen. I love what she does. I like her courage. She really goes for it, and yet at the same time she's vulnerable and feminine and you can make her cry in a minute. I think she's a great actress.

MG: I see that Glenda Jackson is running for Parliament. How do you feel about that?

GAMBON: I don't like that. She's a wonderful actress. Why does she want to give it up?

MG: What do you think about actors in politics?

GAMBON: If you're successful as an actor or actress, you become well known. Why should that indicate that your views are worth listening to? Their views have no more validity than anybody else's.

MG: Some become president of the United States.

GAMBON: If they weren't well known, no-one would listen to them.

MG: You haven't taken public stands.

GAMBON: I've got nothing to say anyway.

MG: But you have opinions.

GAMBON: But why should I express them publicly? As I said before, if you're an actor, the less people know about you the better it is. I don't think you should pander to the public's curiosity. I think it's best to keep a low profile.

It's like a compulsion, isn't it, acting? I don't really like it. I *have* to do it. I've been an actor for almost thirty years, and I can't do without it. It's a release -- something inside you that has to come out. Or maybe you don't know who you are, or maybe you just want to be all sorts of people. That's certainly true of me. I live in a fantasy most of my life. In my offstage life, I'm a pseudo-gunsmith, a pseudo-pilot, a pseudo-expert on this and that. It's all really acting, isn't it? Fundamentally, acting is a deep process of showing off in front of a thousand people, dressing up in costumes and saying, 'Look at me.' That's why the best actors are slightly childish. It's quite a childish thing, acting. Child-like.

MG: Playing games?

GAMBON: Playing games. Yes.

MG: Your chosen career.

GAMBON: Not chosen. It just sort of happens. It did for me anyway. It slowly evolved. It took a long time for me to write on a form: Job? Actor. When I first started at the National, I didn't feel I legitimately belonged. I kept thinking it would come to an end. I'd have to go back and work in a factory. I feel now as though I belong to the theatrical profession.

MG: When did you first feel you might make it as an actor?

GAMBON: It was the play *Events While Guarding the Bofors Gun* [by John McGrath, which he did at the Birmingham Rep] where I played a Northern Ireland Belfast man, quite bright, complex. It was a part really right for me. It sat on me well.

MG: Can acting be taught?

GAMBON: I think you can teach technique. You can certainly listen to tutors. I remember listening to actors talking about what they had learned at drama school. They said you should never just sit on a chair on the stage. You should come over and feel it with the back of your leg, sit on it, but you shouldn't ever look at it. That was the English school of the 1930's stage acting. They don't teach that now.

MG: Now they would probably say, kick the chair over.

GAMBON: They probably don't give a fuck anymore.

MG: Have you ever taught acting?

GAMBON: No. I wouldn't know what to say. I wouldn't be a good teacher. I'd be so cynical. I like to tell people what not to do.

MG: What should an actor not do?

GAMBON: He shouldn't do anything. I'd tell him to cut it all out.

MG: Stop acting?

GAMBON: Stop acting, yes. But then you'd have a whole stage full of people just standing there.

MG: It could be boring.

GAMBON: It could be very boring. So someone would have to start doing something in the end, but it would only be when it had to be done.

MG: There is something different between acting and just 'being'. If you just come onstage, that's not very theatrical.

GAMBON: That's right. The audience would walk out after a half hour. You have to make it interesting. That's what John Dexter used to say: if you had a long speech, you couldn't just do it, blah blah blah, you have to do the middle bit fast then do the end a bit high and gradate it, do machinations with it, give it a bit of fireworks and then take it down. Change the rhythm, and disobey the full stops and commas. It's all that, isn't it?

MG: And all this adds up to your Galileo?

GAMBON: I was not as crude as that, because when you're acting a big part like that, the computer up here is going, 'I did that bit, those last five sentences were quite intense, and now I'm going to do this next bit . . . ' This is the rehearsal process, isn't it? Something you really feel strongly about: punch this couple of lines up, just wake them up. It's not a thought process. It lives in you. It's intuition. That's technique, I suppose.

MG: The cliché is that when an actor is in trouble, he can fall back on technique.

GAMBON: In that case, I'm not much good at technique. I have to find the way the person is.

MG: If you don't find the centre of a character?

GAMBON: I'm lost a bit.

MG: What else should an actor not do? What's bad acting?

GAMBON: Bad acting is just not being real, not being true or believable. You see bad acting everyday in soap operas on television. I do, anyway.

MG: Why do you watch them?

GAMBON: I find them fascinating. That's why people watch the series on at the moment, called *Prisoner Cell Block H*. It's on late at night. Alan Ayckbourn is glued to it. It's just so awful. I've looked at it, but I'm not glued to it.

MG: What do you generally do after a performance?

GAMBON: I go have a drink. Watch a bit of television. You've got to wind down. I go have dinner somewhere. I'll go to Joe Allen. John Dexter used to like the Savoy Grill. He called it The Canteen. I was in the Savoy Grill with him one night. We were just leaving and he stopped at a table on the way out. There was a group of very distinguished men at the table, all in dinner suits. He was talking to this man who was an orchestral conductor. There was a little man sitting here, and I was standing there, waiting for John to finish. This little man looked up at me and said, 'Hello,' and I said, 'Oh hello.' I didn't know who he was, but I knew he was somebody. I said, 'Have you been working?' He said, 'Oh, yes.' I said, 'What do you do?' He said [*adopting a slight European accent*], 'I play the piano.' I said, 'Oh, what's your name?' And he said, 'Arthur Rubinstein.'

MG: I had an interesting conversation with Dennis Potter about you.

GAMBON: I never really spoke to him much. It's hard to know what to say to somebody who's a writer. He's a very sharp man and quite dismissive of people. That's self-evident in the text. I didn't really need to speak to him. It's all there.

MG: We talked about the fact that TriStar wants to make a feature movie out of *The Singing Detective*, an Americanised version. [Eventually that film was made.]

GAMBON: What's the point of that? They're heading for disaster.

MG: The excuse is that many actors play Lear and Willy Loman; why can't two people play *The Singing Detective*?

GAMBON: Because it's not the same. It's a modern television series written for television. There isn't a repeatability factor in that sort of work. I think it's ridiculous. Dennis just wants the money. Can't blame him, I suppose.

MG: Anyway he couldn't have been more admiring of what you did with the role.

GAMBON: Good, because I never spoke to him about it afterwards. He said, 'Well done.' I saw him the night of the award ceremony, when the series didn't win. Dennis was really low. He got steadily pissed, and I said goodbye to him, and I haven't seen him since.

MG: He said your looks were malleable, and that enabled you to change into so many different characters.

GAMBON: I don't look like an actor. I probably look like – I don't know – the manager of a department store.

MG: Today you look like a banker.

GAMBON: Or a solicitor. Or if I'm just wearing old clothes, I look like a gunmaker, I suppose.

MG: Do you worry about your appearance onstage?

GAMBON: Yes, of course. That's why I've never felt right in this play, *Man of the Moment*. I know in my heart for that play really to work, he should be a thinner, shorter man so it would have been more of an event when he charged across that bank all those years ago to grab that gun out of the man's hand. I'm quite a big-boned bloke. There's nothing I can do about it.

MG: Do you work out?

GAMBON: No. I don't believe in it. I don't think you should do anything like that if you don't enjoy it. I believe you get arthritis in your fifties if you do that – someone told me.

MG: Where does your energy come from?

GAMBON: You just invent it.

3 July 1990

'Actors are show-offs, bigheaded bastards, egomaniacs. I can't think of any other reason they act'

Gambon and I met for lunch at Bentley's, an elegant old English institution. He had been there (same table) when he had signed the contract to play Inspector Maigret on television. Today he was not in his banker's suit. Looking around the room at the (real) bankers and barristers, he said, 'I'm the only man here today wearing a lavatory cleaner's jacket.' I said I had seen his agent Larry Dalzell before coming to lunch.

MG: Larry told me how he discovered you when you were playing Othello in Birmingham.

GAMBON: That was the first time Larry saw me. Brian Cox was my Iago, and we'd always been great mates. We did a season together, twelve months, ending with *Othello*. All through the year, he would say to me every week – I'm exaggerating now – but he'd say, 'I'm playing the lead in a big new BBC series called *The Borderers*, where I ride a horse. I start next year.' I said, 'You told me that.' This went on and on. Then one night he said to me, 'They're in tonight: the *Borderers* people.' I said, 'What are they in for if you've got the part?' He said, 'They're just checking up because they've changed the producer.' We did *Othello*, and I'm covered in

104

black and sweating. We were sharing a dressing room, and a knock came on the door. Brian hid behind the door. I opened it, and the man said, 'I'm from the BBC, I'm Peter Graham-Scott, producer of *The Borderers*. I said, 'Brian's here.' He said, 'No, I don't want to speak to him. Would you come out in the corridor for a moment?' I went out in the corridor and there were ten of them, a contingent of producers, and they said, 'Are you interested in playing the lead in a TV series? We'll send you the script in the morning.' That was it. I went back in the dressing room and Brian was there, leaning against the wall. I said, 'I'm sorry, mate.'

MG: He didn't punch you in the nose?

GAMBON: No, he was just depressed.

MG: Then Larry asked you if you had an agent.

GAMBON: I sort of had one, but I wasn't really with her, and she committed suicide a week later.

MG: So Brian didn't get the part, your agent committed suicide, and you went on to fame? Just like an actor.

GAMBON: It was swashbuckling – twenty-six hour-long episodes, two years' work, and it was quite a lot of money. I got to ride a horse and gallop across the lowlands of Scotland.

MG: Could you ride a horse?

GAMBON: I can now, but I didn't then. They sent me to have training with a proper riding school, which was great. One series took seven months to shoot and then we did another seven months the following year. In between the TV series, I played Macbeth at the Forum Theatre in Billingham. And I did some TV plays and a second series of *The Borderers*. Then I went into rep again, at Liverpool, and played Coriolanus and *In Celebration*, the David Storey play about the educated man who comes home to his mother and his miner father. I did the usual double bill, *The Critic* and *Harlequinade*. From there I went to the Royal Shakespeare Company for the first time, in 1970, 1971. I did a season at the Aldwych when Trevor Nunn was running the company. We did Donald Sinden's *Henry VIII*, in which I played the Earl of Surrey, Shaw's *Major Barbara* and Günther Grass's *The Plebeians Rehearse the Uprising*, which Peggy Ashcroft was in. I also did the John Barton adaptation of *Henry IV*, *One and Two* and *Henry V*, condensed into one five-hour evening, called *When Thou Art King*. I played Hotspur in the *Henrys* and then Fluellen in *Henry V*. It was a small production which we took around schools and did it at the Aldwych and then a short run at the Roundhouse.

Then as soon as I finished that stint at the Royal Shakespeare, I got a wonderful part in a TV series, an adaptation of Aldous Huxley's *Eyeless in Gaza*, which I loved, six episodes, part of it shot in Portugal, with Ian Richardson. I did a couple of try-outs of plays and another series for Yorkshire television, called *The Challengers*, with Colin Blakely. This was all before 1974 and *The Norman Conquests*. I see *The Norman Conquests* as a watershed, a moment when I broke through.

MG: In *The Norman Conquests*, there was that absolutely hilarious scene when you were sitting at the table in that low chair. Where did the notion of the 'short chair' come from? Was that your idea, or Alan's?

GAMBON: Oh, that's in the script. They've run out of real chairs, but they have a little baby chair. Tom the vet sits on the chair – you have to play him very straight. He doesn't mind about the low chair when he sits on it. I can't describe it, but there's a technique to getting a laugh on that. It's inside somewhere. If you direct it properly the audience don't initially realise what's happening. Everyone gets seated at table except the lady of the house who's serving the dinner and slowly but surely people in the house see what it is, and it builds up, and it grows and grows and grows and grows.

Ayckbourn wasn't around when we rehearsed it. Things like table settings, who sits where and all that is very important in Ayckbourn. He came in later in rehearsals and we had a few problems around the table scene. He solved it by saying, 'You should be sitting here, she should be sitting there.' It was like a jigsaw puzzle.

MG: The short chair did a lot for you.

GAMBON: Oh, it did. People couldn't stop laughing. That was brilliant. Some nights all six of us would break. We hung on tight, but sometimes during that moment the laughter from the audience was so overwhelming you couldn't carry on with the play. So we would wait. It was like freeze frame. Penny Keith would stand there at one end of the table, and we would just wait until it got down. Then we'd punch in with the next line, and get on with it. I loved that moment. I remember one night at the Globe where we ran in the West End. I'm sitting in the low chair facing the audience. I was looking up and I saw a guy fall out of his seat in the back of the dress circle. [*Fights back laughter and tears.*] He was on an aisle and he was laughing so much that he fell out of his seat and rolled down the gangway.

MG: He was actually rolling in an aisle.

GAMBON: He fell out his seat and rolled down the steps, and I thought, god almighty, brilliant. Moments like that you never forget. That was a wonderful moment. I love that sort of laughter of an audience. The laughter was frightening because they wouldn't stop. They couldn't stop. The house shook. The six of us onstage stopped acting. We waited on the edge, and it was an extraordinary moment. I know why it was so funny. Just the image of a man, quite a big man, sitting eating at a table, with his arms up like that, eating a salad.

MG: Did you laugh?

GAMBON: Oh, Jesus. Yes.

MG: How do you feel about the old Hollywood stars, like Spencer Tracy and James Cagney?

GAMBON: They were brilliant screen actors. They had a wonderful inner clock and knew exactly how to present themselves.

They had discretion and taste and personal integrity. I don't know how they did it. They were just born with it. You don't learn that. I suppose you learn to relax in front of a camera. Bogart – a modern actor, understated. We don't have any more of them. But it's not acting like Olivier in *Richard III.*

MG: Probably Olivier wouldn't have minded having a career like Bogart's.

GAMBON: Thank god it didn't happen because Olivier changed the English theatre. He did *Richard III* and *The Entertainer* and *Othello*, and each one pushed the boundary out, and all the followers came behind him. Olivier and Brando are the two principal 20th-century actors, Brando in film and Olivier in the theatre.

MG: Do you feel more drawn to one than the other?

GAMBON: The fame side and the modern acting side feels more drawn to Brando, but the legitimacy is more drawn to Olivier and the career in the theatre. But the wild man in films is Brando.

MG: When did you see your first Shakespeare?

GAMBON: I didn't see one until I was in one. I'd read *Hamlet* when I was in amateur dramatics. The first Shakespeare I was in was Peter O'Toole's *Hamlet.* And I'd never read *Macbeth* before I played Macbeth.

MG: Not like those Cambridge people who saw it and read it when they were 12.

GAMBON: Well, they were lucky. I'm the unlucky one. But then again, they can't make guns. [*Laughter.*] They wouldn't want to, of course. Their minds are on higher things, on art and literature, creativity and the theatre.

MG: Are actors born liars?

GAMBON: Yes. [For his CV] I used to take all the parts I'd done in the amateur dramatics and just gently move them to a professional theatre. It never did any good, though. Kids

108

still make them up; to get Equity cards they say, 'I played this and that in fringe theatre.' But they can't get Equity cards because Equity doesn't recognise fringe theatre.

Once I wrote a letter full of lies to an agent. I said I'd played the German tutor in *Five Finger Exercise* at Bromley Rep. Blah, blah, blah, blah. He called me into his office. He said, 'You didn't play this part at Bromley Rep because my client Tony Beckley played that and my mother lives in Bromley and I see everything there.' He said, 'You didn't play that other part either. Please don't waste people's time with letters like this.' I stood up and walked out.

MG: How did you feel about O'Toole's Hamlet?

GAMBON: He was magnificent – like a god. He'd just done *Lawrence of Arabia*, and he had bright blond hair. For us, it was wonderful. I don't know about the Hamlet. I wasn't tutored enough to know what was going on. I know that he knew all the lines on the first read-through.

MG: In those days, with O'Toole and Albert Finney, the English theatre was filled with such great promise.

GAMBON: Magnificent! Albert in *Saturday Night and Sunday Morning*. You thought at the time that O'Toole and Finney would be the leaders of this business for the next forty years. In the '60s, we used to go to the Buxton Club, behind the Haymarket. Peter O'Toole, Albert Finney, Richard Harris, Michael Caine. All the actors would go down there every night. It was an actors' club. You had to be a member. One of the challenges was to go round the room without touching the floor.

MG: How did you do that?

GAMBON: On the tops of the chairs.

MG: Which became more and more difficult the more you drank?

GAMBON: Oh, yeah. And there was Jerry's Club on Shaftesbury Avenue, down the basement. But they are all gone.

I suppose young actors go to clubs in Soho, somewhere I don't know about. I lament the loss of all that. I lament Albert Finney not being Sir Albert and running the National Theatre, being what everyone thought he would be.

Maybe I'm just living in cloud cuckooland but during the years when I was at the National in the '60s, we'd go out every night to the Buxton. People have stopped drinking. Maybe they're more health-conscious. They don't smoke, they don't drink, they don't stay out late. It all seems so straightlaced.

I used to hang around with Victor Henry. That was his acting name. He was Alex Henry. You never heard of him? Well, he was a great actor. He was a Royal Court actor; he played all the leads at the Royal Court. Most English actors of my generation revered him. He was a lunatic. Victor Henry – he's dead, got knocked down in a bus queue and went into a coma and lay in a coma for 15 years. His mother and father visited him every day, and we used to go up and talk to him by his bed, and play tapes and videos. He did *Diary of a Madman* in the West End, and he had a video of it – and *The Duchess of Malfi* at the Royal Court.

MG: Are there many actors that you felt might become something extraordinary, and then didn't?

GAMBON: Yes. I've got friends, contemporaries of mine, who I thought were wonderful actors, and they've not done anything. I'll tell you an actor who I think is a tragedy: Nicol Williamson. He was 'The Man' in the '60s. He used to shake up London. People talked about him, he got awards. Where is he now? What does he live on? He was the most superb actor. When he played Bill Maitland in [John Osborne's] *Inadmissible Evidence*, that was the sort of stuff I wanted to do. Tony Richardson directed him in *Hamlet* at the Roundhouse, with Tony Hopkins as Claudius.

MG: He directed himself as Macbeth on Broadway.

GAMBON: Well, he played Macbeth at Stratford with Trevor Nunn directing. Helen Mirren played Lady Macbeth. She told me that one morning there were notes at ten o'clock and Nicol wasn't there and Trevor was tapping his foot. Eventually they saw Nicol walking across the gardens at Stratford an hour late. And he walked in, didn't even say, 'Sorry,' and lay down at the back of the room. Trevor started giving notes. And then this voice suddenly came up: 'Ipswich two, Trevor Nunn.' [*Gambon perfectly imitates Williamson's nasal voice.*] That was his joke, and he kept repeating it, like he was threatening. Where is he? We need a few more like him. Living in the past. I live in the past. I lament it all.

MG: It's interesting what you said before about Sir Albert Finney running the National Theatre.

GAMBON: That's what you would have thought. That wouldn't be out of the question, would it? He obviously didn't want it. That's all there is to it.

MG: I wonder what drives people to become actors?

GAMBON: It's just a compulsion. They have this built-in desire to be somebody else. Actors are show-offs, bigheaded bastards, egomaniacs. I can't think of any other reason they act. Can you?

MG: One might say it's their creative instinct. They're interpretive artists.

GAMBON: Well, yeah. But they're still bigheaded bastards. Interpretive artists – well, they are that as well.

MG: Like musicians. Like Arthur Rubinstein. He was an interpretive artist.

GAMBON: But it didn't matter what Rubinstein looked like. He had a piano, which is a solid thing – and this great skill. He was lucky. Actors don't have . . .

MG: Don't have a piano to play?

GAMBON: No. Actors just have this! [*He points at himself.*] And it's fuck-all they can do about it.

MG: The RSC puts out these books where the actors sit around talking about playing Shakespeare, and there was a TV series, *Playing Shakespeare*. John Barton leads the sessions.

GAMBON: He's a great teacher. I've worked with him, a good man, a great scholar and a wonderful teacher. I don't pooh-pooh all that, but I find it a bit boring when you read books or see TV programmes about it. In my experience at Stratford, you can work on the text forever, but they'll put an explosion behind you. Bob Peck played Macbeth with a band behind him. He's standing there in a pair of braces. 'Is this the dagger I see before me? The handle towards my hand.' And he's doing that, and there's a bloke behind him with a drum on a raised platform, going like that. Boom, boom. I saw that happen. A lot of directors don't trust actors. I believe Deborah Warner isn't like that. I believe she's excellent.

MG: Often she strips the stage, brings it back to basics.

GAMBON: Great clarity. No bullshit. That German director, Peter Stein. His lighting is quite astonishing. Lights can be so wonderful. [*Suddenly.*] You can't park your car at Stratford.

MG: If they said, what's your wish, you would say, a parking space?

GAMBON: A parking space. That was the first question when I rang up Scarborough: Is there a space to park the car? It's like a weight around your neck. I was looking yesterday at the new Toyota Luxor, which has been an enormous hit in America. It's just the most fantastic car. It's 34,000 quid, and it has every-thing: air-conditioning, cruise control, quadrophonic sound, compact disc player, analogue dashboard, every single thing for that money. It's got lever memory seats. Memory seats! If someone else drove it, they'd adjust the seats to suit them-selves, but when you got back in, you'd press your number – teet, teet – and the whole seat would revert back to your position. The mirrors would move to you – vrrrrm – and you can have four settings. As you open the door and pull the

112

ignition key out, the steering wheel goes bzzzzt. It moves up to clear your legs and let you get out.

Did you see the football on Saturday? Cameroon? We were disgraceful. It was shocking to watch. I think we're going to get murdered on Wednesday.

MG: Did you ever play football?

GAMBON: I did at school. I was a left-back. That means you don't have to do anything. I quite like following football. I love cricket.

MG: Do you admire athletes?

GAMBON: Yes, I do. I like one-to-one athletes, tennis players, runners, things like that. I'm not too sure about the big team games. I like to watch a football team really work in unison, as a group. The sharing, the sweeping movement when the ball goes up the field – it's like eleven men working for one end. That's rare. Tennis is like the old tournaments: knights in armour. Women's tennis is deeply sexy. Invariably lady tennis players are beautiful, aren't they? I don't know why that is. Maybe the athletic body has to be a certain shape.

MG: Sometimes tennis players are not natural athletes: they have to work hard to be good. Some actors are like that.

GAMBON: They teach themselves. I suppose Sir Laurence worked at it.

MG: Acting's a lot of hard work.

GAMBON: Hard slog and heartache and misery – for moments of sheer joy. For *Galileo* – to hear your friends clapping. And *View from the Bridge*, when we came off the first night, Alan Ayckbourn was in the wings, crying. I was quite moved.

5 July 1990

'You go over the top, don't you?'

Last night after the theatre, I met Gambon at Joe Allen's. I arrived at 11, and he was already there, sitting by himself. He said that on Saturday he was meeting his Iago, the designer and Ayckbourn to begin preparing for late August rehearsal of Othello. *We spoke about his various projects. Then he told a story about Duncan Weldon, who had offered him a very small salary to do* Old Times *in the West End, and when Gambon objected, he said it was the same amount of money that Rex Harrison was currently making at the Haymarket Theatre for the play preceding* Old Times. *So Gambon marched over to the Haymarket and went backstage to see Harrison. Gambon said that he was an actor and Harrison said, 'Yes, I know. I've seen you.' 'I'm doing a play here after you, with Duncan Weldon.' 'That cheap bastard!' Harrison said. 'Is he giving you trouble?' Gambon explained about the salary, and Harrison said that yes he was getting that, but also a suite at the Dorchester, a chauffeur-driven car and other perks. When Gambon reported that back to Weldon, the producer fumed but increased his salary.*

Finishing the meal, he said goodbye to some actors at a rear table, and tapped the pianist on the shoulder and thanked him. With his rhythmic, swinging walk, he took two steps at a time as he left the restaurant.

The next day at 1 p.m. I was at Dalzell's office to meet Gambon. He had gone to Earl's Court to be fitted with coloured contact lenses for Othello, *and was caught in traffic. Our meeting was postponed to before the performance that evening. We sat in his dressing room.*

MG: Peter Hall said he could imagine you as a strolling player.

GAMBON: Oh, yes. Going round. Pair of old trousers, sleeping on the floor. I'd like that. I couldn't do it now because you get too comfortable when you're middle-aged. If it's an older man, it's rather sad. To a certain extent, a strolling player means an unsuccessful one.

MG: Did you always feel the urge to show off?

GAMBON: Yes. I've always been a liar. I think all children fib. That's part of the excitement of being a child. I remember fantasising with my friends at school, with one particular friend. We would tell each other what our daddies did, and what our mums did. All lies. I'd say, my father had gone to Africa. Children know. You enter into a pact, a game.

MG: Did you feel any trepidation when you quit your job at the factory?

GAMBON: I didn't quit until I got the job in Ireland with Micheál MacLiammóir that I told you about. The weekend before I was to start in Dublin, I packed the job in, and off I went.

MG: And haven't been out of work since?

GAMBON: No. When I came back from Ireland, which was only two months, I had a bit of a lean time. I told you I was in a Christmas show at the Mermaid, and then I was an assistant stage manager/understudy in the West End. I went on for an actor called Bob Todd. He wanted a night off because of the BBC television, so he gave me a pound to go on for him. But I had to keep my mouth shut. He said he was ill. You're not supposed to do that.

MG: And that was your West End debut?

GAMBON: Yes, West End debut. You won't believe what I had to do. I had to stand on the top of a stepladder. This was Spike Milligan playing the lead in *The Bedsitting Room* [in January

1963 at the Mermaid]. Standing on the top of the stepladder, I was wearing army boots, a Nazi steel helmet and a string vest, and I sang a song about washing powder: 'When I Was a Young Man My Vest Was Always Dirty.' I normally operated the sound in the wings during the run.

While I was in that show, I had the freedom to go to those classes at the Royal Court where I met Bill Gaskill. They weren't acting classes as such, they were really improvisation classes, mime and mask work. Later we had a mime teacher at the National, called Claude Chagrin, when we did *The Royal Hunt of the Sun.* There was a lot of mime in that production. We had to climb the Andes. We also had a voice teacher at the National. I suppose indirectly there was quite a lot of teaching there.

MG: Until I heard you imitating Nicol Williamson, I wasn't aware of you as a mimic.

GAMBON: I'm not a good mimic. To be a good mimic, you've got to be able to do anything as the person. I mean anyone can do Marlon Brando in *The Godfather.* [*He mumbles as Brando in* The Godfather], but you've got to be able to do Marlon Brando having his breakfast.

MG: How did you feel about *The Cook, the Thief, His Wife and Her Lover*?

GAMBON: When I read the script, I found it sidesplittingly funny. He wrote it for you to laugh at, and he wanted to upset you as well. I was amazed when I saw it in a cinema and people sat there silently. I would imagine the audience would be in an uproar. I'm sure that's what Greenaway wanted.

MG: That character is certainly the most monstrous man you've played.

GAMBON: Yes, he is. It was wonderful to play such a horrible bastard. Such grotesque behavior! Tipping that tureen of soup over the man's head, kneeing the bloke in the bollocks when he was having a pee. It was like out of a cartoon strip, like a kid being let loose in a playpen. I smashed the kitchen up, didn't I? Throw milk, meat, sausages, tomatoes, throw them all, pans, boiling water. Create fucking havoc! [*All this said very gently.*] You can only do it once. It was a low-budget film. They didn't have double things: glass bottles, great carboys of milk. I said to Greenaway, 'What the fuck am I going to do?' He said, 'Just do it. We'll stay with you in the track, but try and make it smooth.' So we started it and I went berserk.

Greenaway advertised for five hundred extras in *The Times*. All these people turned up. There was one big eating scene. They were sitting at these tables, but they weren't told what I was going to do. We rehearsed before they got on to the set. They came in wearing their beautiful dresses and carrying chihuahuas. They were all very excited to be in the film. And then: 'Silence in the studio! Action!' [*He claps like a clapboard.*] These people were totally taken by surprise. I took the tablecloth and whopped it off the table. It nearly misfired in the lavatory scene. Greenaway had a series of women sitting in the cubicles. He said, 'This man's going to kick each door in and drag you all out.' He said, 'Action,' and it wasn't at all like I said I'd do it. You go over the top, don't you? I opened one cubicle and started throwing stuff out: brooms, pails, buckets. I had been told not to throw the last bucket because it was made of steel. Fucking massive thing! But I couldn't stop myself. I could hardly lift it. I threw it like this. [*He heaves the imaginary bucket.*] It went through the air. It was a great shot because it went straight past the lens of the camera. But it could have smashed that £50,000 camera. [*He slaps an imaginary clapboard.*] Greenaway said, 'Print!'

MG: Where does all that violence come from?

GAMBON: It has nothing to do with violence. The character's wife is double-crossing him. So he goes berserk. You'd like to do that. You'd love to break up a kitchen – just for fun.

117

Interlude

During the next dozen years, Gambon finally began to have a film career, with *A Man of No Importance*, *The Gambler*, *Last September*, *Dancing at Lughnasa*, *The Insider* and *Gosford Park*. He also acted in some challenging television projects, including *Wives and Daughters*, *Longitude* and Stephen Poliakoff's *Perfect Strangers* (also known as *Almost Strangers*), for which he won three BAFTA awards in a row. In *Path to War*, he played Lyndon Johnson. At the same time, as always, he was busy in the theatre. In May 1995 he starred in David Hare's *Skylight* at the National Theatre and the following year brought it to New York for his Broadway debut. That was followed by *Tom and Clem*, *Cressida* and a revival of *The Caretaker*. I saw all four plays in London and *Skylight* again in New York. Often when I was in London, he and I would meet. During this time, he was knighted by Prince Charles.

I first saw *Skylight* at the National in June 1995. In this three-character play, Gambon played Tom Sergeant, a rich restaurateur and a buccaneer of industry. He had risen by his own bootstraps, and along the way, had lost a certain sense of humanity. Ostensibly a play about the relationship between Gambon's character and his young mistress (played by Lia Williams), *Skylight* also dealt with class war. As an actor's vehicle, it was a tour de force for both Gambon and Williams.

On July 4, Gambon and I met for lunch. He was in rehearsal for *Volpone*, co-starring Simon Russell Beale, soon to open at the National. We went to Cranks health-food restaurant near the rehearsal hall. It was self-service, and as Gambon walked along carrying his tray, with a chef's salad on it, the tray nearly tipped over. He saved it just in time, and did so with the gracefulness of a Chinese gymnast. I said that if he hadn't, it would have been like a scene in a farce. 'I couldn't repeat it,' he said, with a smile. We talked about *Volpone*, a real farce, directed by Matthew Warchus. He said he was having a good time so far, which was not entirely the case with *Skylight*. Because of all the arguments between his character and the one played by Lia Williams, it was a difficult role to play and he didn't finish a performance feeling happy. As was evident, the actors carried the play, and he knew he had a good role. He said that prior to this he had turned down Hare's *Absence of War*, and then the playwright offered him *Skylight*. Gambon said that he thought Hare may have written it with him in mind because of the reference to the character's 'big hands'.

Skylight was a great success. He said the plan was to do it with *Volpone* in repertory at the National until the end of the year, then transfer it to the West End. He said he was glad that he was doing the two plays and remembered telling me when I was writing the profile that he wanted to do a classic and a new play at the same time. He made several references to 'the article in the *New Yorker*,' saying that it had bought him his new house. The house was in Kent, about a half hour from London, and it was, he said, an estate, complete with a pool and a six-car garage. And six cars? 'That's when I really become a star,' he said.

When he went to Los Angeles, he said, the profile was sitting on the producer's desk. That was, I suggested, the kiss of death. No, he said, the opposite. That and *The Cook, the Thief* brought him a healthy amount of film work, at least for a time. Now, he said, after several flops (like *Toys*), his film career was over (not so).

In the fall of 1996, Gambon made his Broadway debut in *Skylight*, again directed by Richard Eyre. The play opened to favourable reviews, especially so for Gambon and Lia Williams. On Sunday 29 September, Gambon came to our house for dinner after the matinee performance. The other guests included Al Hirschfeld who, when asked, talked about Charlie Chaplin, William Saroyan and others who had passed through his life.

Gambon listened attentively and also spoke about the difficulty of sustaining his performance. He hoped that the play would finish its run on schedule in December and not be extended. He was eager to get on with his next project, *Tom and Clem*, a play about Clement Atlee (to be played by Alec McCowen) and Tom Driberg, a homosexual Member of Parliament and a vivid London personality (Gambon). The author was Stephen Churchett, better known as an actor. Unsolicited, he had left the play at the office of Michael Codron. It happened to be on top of a stack of scripts when the producer came in the next day. He read it, Gambon said, and immediately decided to do it. He rang up the actors, and, in a very short space of time, the play was scheduled to open in the West End. Gambon also talked about *The Cook, the Thief*, and said that when he described his role in it to Olivier, Olivier said, 'Forget it. I'll do it.'

The next few weeks in New York, Gambon made the rounds of the television and radio talk shows. On 25 October, he and I met for lunch at the Players. He said that he had a dream project. It was to be about a seedy detective he knew who operated out of a phone booth in Leicester Square, and wore a dirty raincoat and did mostly divorce cases. Gambon knew him because he used movie stuntmen as assistants. This was, he thought, the world's worst detective. Sounded like a role for Peter Sellers – or Michael Gambon.

My wife and I saw *Tom and Clem* in London in June. Having been warned that this was a play more of interest to the English than to Americans, I was pleasantly surprised. The meeting between Atlee and Driberg was manufactured but proved to be dramatic and also highly comic, because of the twinned performances of the two stars. Gambon threw himself into the role of Driberg, as if to bad manners born. He and McCowen were engaging opposites, as Gambon's Driberg opened himself to his obsessions (political and social liberalism) and McCowen's Atlee remained the quiet compromiser. Gambon played this outrageous and flamboyant homosexual with great panache. He may have already been tired of the role, but he certainly did not show it onstage. After the performance, we went round to congratulate him. I telephoned him the next day. He said he was enjoying the show, but it was not doing well. The good reviews brought in business for the first weeks, but then it sloughed off. He thought that perhaps people were tired of politics, or at least of political theatre.

Back again in London in April of 2000 – and Gambon was onstage in Nicholas Wright's *Cressida*. In it, he played an actor-manager in Shakespearean times, buying, training and selling boy actors to play women's roles in the theatre. The play was slight, but Gambon tackled his role with zest, and had one wonderful scene in which he educated one boy in the ways and means of performance. It was a superb Elizabethan acting class. Backstage after the show, he was in high spirits. He introduced me to the author and said he had never been in a happier company.

He had also just done *Endgame* with David Thewlis as part of the television series filming all Beckett's stage plays. He talked about the television film in which he would play Lyndon Johnson and said he was concerned about doing a Texan accent. I suggested lunch early the following week, but he said that he was busy having his portrait painted for the National Portrait Gallery, 'if they buy it.'

In November of 2000, Gambon returned to Pinter, playing Davies in a West End revival of *The Caretaker* at the Comedy Theatre, a production directed by Patrick Marber. Gambon was the shabbiest, seediest Davies imaginable, which made him all the more amusing as he asserted his 'dignity'. There had been talk about extending the run and perhaps moving it to Broadway, but those plans were abandoned.

In March 2002, we were in London again and drove down to the West End to see Simon Russell Beale in *Humble Boy*. As usual, I stopped my car at a single yellow line on a street near the theatre to wait there until 6.30 when the parking regulations went off. I looked up – and who was that standing in front of our car, spiffily dressed in a dark blue suit and talking on a mobile? It was Michael Gambon. I got out of the car and startled him. He said into his phone, 'Here I am in the middle of the street – and here's Mel.' He was on his way to the opening of his new movie, *Ali G Indahouse*, starring Ali G, the white British comic character who pretends to be black. In the film Gambon played the British prime minister. We chatted for a few minutes about that movie and also about his upcoming role as Lyndon Johnson on television. Then off he went to his premiere – and we to the theatre. Coincidentally, Gambon's 'friend' Prince Charles was in the audience that night. He was seeing Russell Beale, and not Ali G.

In September 2002, Gambon took up the challenge of acting in Caryl Churchill's *A Number*, a futuristic play about the hazards of cloning and parenting. In it, he played a man in his early sixties, who is confronted by a clone of his son, his actual son and another clone, all played by a single actor, David Craig, with no change of costume and a scant change of sensibility. This made the play something of a mystery, and also placed a great burden on the actors to differentiate – and illuminate – the various roles. Because of his failure in bringing up his son, the father tries to do it all over again – with negligible, if not disastrous, results. I saw the play (in Stephen Daldry's production at the Royal Court) on 12 November and thought it was one of Churchill's most disturbing and penetrating plays, one that encouraged Gambon – who was onstage for the entire sixty minutes – to dig deeply within himself.

Afterwards, we went backstage and congratulated him. At my request he cleared up the question of the sons – the sequence and difference. I praised the scene in which he collapses on the floor in tears, and then a spiral of cigarette smoke rises: an artfully contradictory picture of a man torn between compassion for his son and callousness. He said, with a certain pride, 'That's mine,' indicating that part of his challenge was finding aspects of character to play between the lines.

Several days later, I interviewed Simon Russell Beale at the Donmar Warehouse, then walked over to Orso to have lunch with Gambon. It was not yet 2 p.m., but Gambon was already there, sitting at a table in the back and smoking a cigarette. He had just come from doing a voice-over commercial, which he had had to repeat several times. Yes, he still needed to do voice-overs for the money, and felt no embarrassment about it.

We talked about *A Number*, which was closing that weekend. He said that it was too difficult and too intense to do for a longer run, but it might reopen later in the West End or on Broadway – perhaps a year from then. He said that the play grew out of a nightmare that Caryl Churchill had had, in which her grandson was abused (not true). As with Pinter, she would not explain or analyse the play for the actors. In the text, there are no stage directions, so the actors added to it. Gambon said that Pinter came to see the play but didn't go round after the performance. 'He didn't like it,' Gambon concluded. I said that he did, and told me the performance was one of Gambon's best. The actor seemed happy at that thought.

I told him about my talk with Russell Beale, with whom he co-starred in *Volpone* at the National Theatre. Though the actors are of different generations and have different approaches to acting, they greatly admire one another and are friends. I said that Russell Beale was thinking about doing Brecht's *Galileo*, which was one Gambon's greatest successes. He said that he wanted to play 'a man of faith,' but hesitated about *Galileo*, because Gambon had done it. Gambon said that was a while ago, and why shouldn't he do it? Then he paused and grinned. 'That son of a bitch!' He said that he enjoyed working with Russell Beale in *Volpone* and, in typical fashion, had tried to corpse him. I said that Russell Beale indicated that after *Volpone*, he had become 'less puritanical' about his performing. Gambon said that if he had helped him, he was pleased.

21 November 2002

'If I had been born again, I'd be a ballet dancer'

I arrived at noon, early for our meeting, at the National Theatre, and Gambon was sitting at the espresso bar having a coffee with a friend. 'See you at 12.30,' he said. About fifteen minutes later, I was in the lobby leafing through a new biography of Alan Ayckbourn when Gambon appeared. We went up to the Terrace Café for lunch, and sat by the window, looking out towards the Thames. He was smartly dressed in a blue suit. He had just completed the limited run in A Number, *and for this moment he was between assignments.*

MG: On the front page of today's *Telegraph*, it said that you were at St James's Palace for an event with Prince Charles. Alan Bates and Penelope Keith were there too. In the story it said that Charles had acted in the Scottish play at school.

GAMBON: He was very funny. He's a very funny man. He gave a speech which went on for about five minutes, and had the whole room roaring with laughter. He said he was a terrible actor. One time when he was a little boy, his guardian took him to the Royal Opera House and introduced him to the ballet. Then he was taken to the Old Vic to see *Twelfth Night*, and The Crazy Gang at the Victoria Palace. When he was at school, he was cast as Macbeth, and his mum and dad came to see it. There's one bit where Macbeth's going mad, and he dreams. He said it was going very well, until he heard this man laughing. It was his dad laughing at him. After, he said, 'Why the hell were you laughing?' His dad said, 'Well it's just so ridiculous. You're a terrible actor.'

MG: That's why he didn't become an actor.

GAMBON: Yes, yes.

MG: I can't imagine him doing Macbeth.

GAMBON: Oh, no. Terrible. But he said he's always loved the theatre. I'm sure he does. His nanny used to take him out at night without anyone knowing. She'd smuggle him out of Buckingham Palace, and take him to see all the shows.

MG: Has he seen you act?

GAMBON: Yes, he has. He said to me yesterday that he came to the premiere of that terrible film, *Charlotte Gray*. He said, 'What did you think of that?' I said that I didn't like it. He said, 'No, I didn't like it much. But I can't say it out loud. I can't pass a judgment on anything.'

MG: So Charles is a film critic.

GAMBON: Yeah. Actor, film critic, ballet dancer.

MG: What was the event at the Palace?

GAMBON: It was the 150th anniversary of the Actors' Benevolent Fund, which was set up by Henry Irving to help poor and destitute actors, and it still exists today.

MG: There are still poor and destitute actors?

GAMBON: There are more now. If you're poor and destitute and you're 60, you can go to them and they'll give you money. You have to prove that you're in trouble. When it goes a bit wrong, I can go and get some [*laughs*] money. I couldn't do that. I'd rather beg in the streets than admit defeat.

The theatre is not like it was when I started acting. It's changed. When I started being an actor, it was quite classy. The Old Vic and Sir Laurence and Sir Ralph. We don't have that now. It's gone.

MG: You're playing some of the same roles that they did.

GAMBON: I'm very subjective about it all. I can't be objective. When we were at the Old Vic with Sir Laurence, if he spoke to you, you would go and tell someone what he said to you. It was that big a deal. You'd go home and say, 'Sir Laurence spoke to me. He said hello.' It was something really alarming. Big! But now . . .

MG: Now, actors go home and say, 'Sir Michael spoke to me. He said hello.'

GAMBON [*fighting back the laughter*]: I don't think so. If they do, I don't know about it.

MG: Olivier probably knew about it.

GAMBON: He might have.

MG: Whenever I interviewed him, he was interesting and coherent, but when I heard him speak at an event, you couldn't follow what he was saying.

GAMBON: Just speaking, not acting? He couldn't get to the point. I think he was just nervous. I had to do a speech the other week onstage at Greenwich University, just saying thank you for a degree. I've never been so frightened in my life. I stood up on the platform and said, 'Sorry, I can't do this. I've stood on stages all over the world and made speeches from Shakespeare and Chekhov, but I've never done this before. I haven't got a script.'

MG: Without a script, it's you.

GAMBON: I don't want to be that.

MG: You could assume a role of someone accepting a degree.

GAMBON: But you have to rehearse it. You'd have to know the proper thing to say. I should have had someone write out a speech and gone through it with me. Instead I made a mess of it, and I stood there like a bumbling idiot, and said something about not having a script, and how nervous I was, instead of facing up to it. If that ever happens again, I'll do it properly.

MG: When you're onstage as yourself, that's it?

GAMBON: I can't do it. I'm nervous. I don't have any confidence. I don't know what to say. I can't improvise. I can't express my thoughts. Whenever I receive awards, I muck that up. The last time I received an award in London was disgraceful. I won the Evening Standard Award. It was a big event at the Savoy Hotel, and I had a few drinks. Maggie Smith was presenting me with Actor of the Year. It was for *Volpone* and *Skylight* and all that stuff, and I went up, took the statue off her. I turned around to the audience. My heart was pounding, and I said – out loud – 'Wow, fuck me!' And there was a pause, and suddenly the whole audience went up laughing. And I said, 'Thank you very much,' and walked off. It was disgraceful. Some older actor said to me afterward, 'You should be ashamed of yourself. You're bringing this profession into disrepute.' If I ever get another one, I'll get a professional writer to write something. I've never done things properly. I always leave things to the last minute. A bit like acting.

MG: As you say that, I remember the scene in Stephen Poliakoff's television series *Perfect Strangers*, when you get up and give your speech at that reunion. The character is almost out of control.

GAMBON: He was out of control, and he has a minor stroke towards the end of it. Doing TV or films, you can't really rehearse it, in the way that we do plays. You stand in front of the audience, and you think, I hope something happens here, and luckily it does. I wait until it comes, and then . . . let it go, and whatever technique you have, a combination of potluck and stagecraft, something can come out of it. You hit the jackpot, and the thing goes bang! And it takes off. Then you can do that the next night. You can remember what it was like. That's what it's all about – trying different things in the rehearsal room. I do that in front of an audience to a certain extent. I can change things quite drastically in front of an audience. That's why I find it difficult to talk about acting, because I do it on the moment. I went to a drama school at New York University to talk to students when I was in

Skylight in New York. The five hundred students who were there must have been very confused. I had nothing to say really. I said, 'Ask me questions and I'll try to answer them.' They asked me how I got ready for a part, what preparation I do, how I went through the rehearsal process. Though I answered all those questions, I wasn't very interesting.

I said, for me acting was mainly instinct – instinct if you get it right, then it solidifies, and then you use it. As John Dexter used to say to me, 'Never do two speeches the same. Always vocally keep a change going all the time.' Even though that might not be implied in the text. But it makes acting more interesting to watch.

MG: And these things would mainly come in rehearsal?

GAMBON: Yeah. Occasionally onstage, and then you make use of it.

MG: Yes. Did you coin that phrase, 'acting is shouting in the night?'

GAMBON: It's just a joke, really. I've got a good loud voice, and in the Olivier Theatre, which is a big one, which I love, you really do have to give it some force to be heard, whereas in front of the film camera, you can just whisper, can't you? Compared to film acting, stage acting is shouting in the night.

MG: Film acting is whispering in the daytime?

GAMBON: Whispering in the daytime. Stage acting is walking on a tightrope and film acting is walking on a white chalk line on the floor.

MG: Would you prefer it if the theatre now was like it was then?

GAMBON: I would, because there's no way now for you to pick up this trade in England. All the reps, the provincial theatres have closed. They're shut down. There's no money left. Theatres employ actors play by play. There's no such thing as what I used to do, be in a company, and just play as cast. That seems to have all gone. I think that's a tragedy for young people. Today you really do have to go to drama school. There's nowhere you could do that, sit around for three years watching people.

MG: Could we talk about *A Number*, and how it came about?

GAMBON: When I read the play, I didn't want to do it. But then Stephen [Daldry] luckily pushed me a bit, and I read it again, and finally I said yes, and I'm glad I did, because it's an intriguing, wonderful exercise for me – to play that part. And I found that after we opened I made quite big changes in my approach to it. I tried to make the character more rounded, give him more of an expanse. For the first week or so, I was a bit flat, I think. I didn't give enough variation with each son, in each of the five scenes. So after a few weeks I found myself playing that man sort of very different in each scene, or it seemed to be very different from my point of view. I quite like the digging that goes on in performance.

MG: In her script, Churchill gives very little information to the actor. There is practically no punctuation in the dialogue.

GAMBON: The sections where there are big breakdowns and collapsing on the stage, and screaming, that's nowhere in the text. You can find an indication of it in the stress of the words. The man is obviously distressed.

MG: How do you do the breakdown? Did Daldry say, 'Now it's time to break down?'

GAMBON: No, I just did that one day in rehearsal. I just did it like that! Maybe not the same as in performance. But they said, 'We like that. Keep it in.'

MG: That's a very dramatic scene.

GAMBON: Oh, yes. It seemed to require something really big to happen.

MG: But the playwright and the director apparently didn't know that until it was done.

GAMBON: I don't think they knew it until I suddenly did it one day in rehearsal, and they thought, oh, that works. I think that's a good way of working. In that Christopher Hampton play, *Tales from Hollywood*, the character dies by a tree falling on his head in the Champs Elysées. I have a long speech to the audience about how I was walking down the Champs Elysées and this tree falls – and suddenly in rehearsal I just collapsed. Boom! Enormous!

MG: Like a tree falling.

GAMBON: Yes. And I did it in rehearsal, and I always did it after that. Peter Gill, the director, said, that's good, it's a visual. I like to physicalise things. That's what I'm talking about. It's physicalising acting. The way you stand or the way you fall, and to do things that are surprising, that shocks an audience. In *Skylight*, I did a scene with Lia [Williams] where I'm talking normally to her about my wife. And in rehearsal one day, I suddenly broke down in tears. We always kept that in.

MG: How do you break down in tears? Technique?

GAMBON: Initially it's not. You get the feeling of what the man's going through, with his dead wife. In rehearsal when this thing suddenly happens, it's real. Then of course it can't be real every night. You learn the feeling of it, and the physicality of it.

MG: Is it like The Method? You look within yourself?

GAMBON: Yes. You play the reality of what's been written.

MG: From your own life?

GAMBON: No, no.

MG: In *A Number*, did you think about yourself and your son?

GAMBON: No, never. I don't know where it comes from. It's imagination, I suppose. Or a feeling of how one would feel in that situation.

MG: Not how one felt, but how one would feel.

GAMBON: Would feel, yes. I think so. The only thing I've ever done like that is in plays when I'm about to burst out laughing, and don't want to, or am not allowed to. And I've been in that situation. I'm prone to do that. Then I think of the image of the girl in Vietnam – this is a bit excessive – with the napalm, the girl running down the street with no clothes on. I've always found that *so* distressing. Every time I think of it, it makes me cry. [*He fights back tears.*] When I've been in plays where I'm about to burst out laughing, I think of that girl. And I don't laugh.

MG: And the opposite – is there something funny you think of when you want to laugh?

GAMBON: That never works. I think that's the most difficult thing an actor has to do – to laugh. You know that famous stage direction, 'Enter laughing.' It's virtually impossible. Well, there are technical actors who can do it. I couldn't do it. I'd find some way around it.

MG: 'Enter crying' you could do?

GAMBON: I could do 'Enter crying,' yes. That would be easier for me. Easier for most people, I think. But I wouldn't really be crying. I'd be just physically showing it. I'd have my face covered up because of my hands.

MG: 'Exit laughing'?

GAMBON: That'd be easier.

MG: The scene in *A Number*, where you fall on the floor, and then we see the spiral of cigarette smoke rising. You're smoking.

GAMBON: Yes. We just did it. I just thought it would be funny. When I'm rehearsing plays, I always think what it looks like, the picture the audience is seeing. When I'm rehearsing, I can see somewhere in here [*he points to his head*], what they're going to see. In *A Number*, when I'm with my son, I spend a

131

lot of time like that, right up close. It looks very odd. But I thought, that's a good closeness. It's sort of stylised, isn't it? Then with the scene on the floor, I kept thinking, maybe these look like letters of the alphabet. [*He illustrates with his hands.*] You've got one man standing like that, and one man there. If one man puts his hand out like that, it's the letter H. That's Daniel Craig and me. We're like that, sometimes close, then we separate. If I go in to touch him, it's a letter H. When I fall on the floor, he's standing, and I'm lying down. It's the letter L. And so I thought in the smoking scene, because I've got my back to the audience – they're very quiet because it's quite dramatic there; he's cried and he falls down – and then suddenly after quite a long pause, the smoke starts rising. I think that's a great image. Also it makes the audience laugh.

MG: What does it say about the character?

GAMBON: It says that he's becoming hysterical, he's fallen down, he's full of remorse, and then he stops crying and he says, 'Christ, I need a cigarette.' Isn't that it? Which if you smoke, you probably do. It's legitimate, isn't it?

MG: Doesn't it also show a certain emotional coldness, contradicting what came just before?

GAMBON: That's a plus then, if that's the case. That crossed my mind. I don't mind that. The fact that he can cut off, which might explain his behaviour with the real child, the way he got rid of it.

MG: That was a difficult play to do?

GAMBON: Oh, really tough. We did just about enough of it. That's why doing a commercial run of a play like that doesn't seem right. It seems to have its own little life. To do it for two months in the Royal Court seems enough.

MG: Why was it harder than other plays?

GAMBON: I suppose because not many things are ever really settled in it. Both Daniel and I felt we were sort of standing on water, that every night was different. That you had a certain freedom to do what you wanted to do every night. Somehow that doesn't lend itself to a run.

MG: But also the play itself is so underwritten.

GAMBON: And you have to bring so much to it. It seemed in rehearsal to be a play that needed a lot of stuff on top, a lot of physicality, which had to do with closeness. Yes, it is underwritten.

MG: How closely did you work with Caryl Churchill? Was she at rehearsals?

GAMBON: She was there every day. She would make comments. She was always very helpful and I think she liked what we did. It's nice to have the writer there.

MG: Would she ever rewrite a line?

GAMBON: No. Maybe one line. A bit like Harold [Pinter] – she wouldn't touch it. Whereas when I worked with David Hare, David rewrites quite drastically. He'll rewrite a whole scene overnight and come in the next day with a different scene.

MG: Could we talk about *The Caretaker*? I gather that you and Patrick Marber [who directed the revival, with Gambon in the title role] didn't get along.

GAMBON: I like Patrick and I wouldn't like to say things about him. There wasn't much of a work ethic in the rehearsal room, I suppose. I've always wanted directors to guide me and tell me what to do, to work out a formal structure. We were very loose in that rehearsal room. I couldn't learn the lines, and it all seemed to run away from me. When we opened, it was a hit, and we were packed. It was a complete surprise to me. I thought, how is this ever going to work? I went right over the top in that one with my physicality. I found I couldn't play the part if I was taller than Rupert [Graves] or Douglas [Hodge]. That tramp is not a big man. I'm big. So I played

133

him with a *severe* stoop. I was never above either of them. That man has to look up at people. That's his insinuating quality. I can't see how you can play him tall. And also I tried to make him as physically repulsive as I could – dirty! So if you do that, if you happen to know the lines, and you stoop and you're dressed in rags and you have the structure that's so formal in Harold's plays, you can't go far wrong.

MG: When you came onstage, you were so repulsive, the audience seemed to shrink away – as if they could smell you. It was more than physicality. It was olfactory.

GAMBON: I used my very big hands in that. So I was stooped and I've got very long arms and long fingers. I used to keep my fingers fully extended down by the side of my trousers. I imagine it used to look grotesque because you've got this stooping man, with these enormous arms, and out of the bottom of jacket come these enormous hands. Someone who had seen it said to me, 'Were they false hands that you have?'

MG: But you do like a director to help you.

GAMBON: I do. That wasn't a happy experience. It wasn't too bad when we opened and it started running. But I've never disliked a rehearsal period more than that. I just couldn't get it going. I know I let Harold down.

MG: Was Harold there at rehearsal?

GAMBON: No, he wasn't. It was a strange experience – very depressing.

MG: People didn't notice. The production got good reviews. It probably could have moved to Broadway.

GAMBON: Yes. You didn't know. Would critics know a good production from a bad one? I don't know. No, they didn't know. We managed to pull the wool over their eyes. But then when I was in a moment of despair, you think, well, Harold says, 'Man sits on bed. He stands. He moves to the gas cooker. He gets out a penknife.' Then I think to myself, does this play need a director? Whatever you do is there in that room. He almost tells you what to do. But of course it does need a director. It does, it does, like mad.

MG: All plays need directors?

GAMBON: They do. Actors need directors. To create a structure. And I've been lucky the last few years with directors. I worked twice with Matthew Warchus. I did the Yasmina Reza play [*The Unexpected Man*] in the West End with Eileen [Atkins] and I did *Volpone* [with Simon Russell Beale] here at the National. They were both with Matthew. They were really enjoyable – terrific stuff. And I did a production of Nick Wright's new play, *Cressida*, with Nick Hytner directing. I liked that experience.

MG: That was a very odd play.

GAMBON: Yes. Some good moments in it. Lovely little rich bits where you could get your teeth into it. I liked the scene in which the older man, myself, teaches the younger boy about stage acting.

MG: That was the best scene in the play.

GAMBON: I thought that was moving and beautiful.

MG: You could use that when you teach acting at NYU or some other place. Just go into the scene.

GAMBON: Yes!

MG: You have the reputation of changing things in a long run.

GAMBON: Some long runs I've been in, you never see the director again. The director seems to disappear on the first night – and that's it. He gets paid of course, but he never comes back to see you. So the play wobbles more and gets more off-course, and begins to meander all over the place. The original play you rehearsed disappears because there's not this figure around to keep his hand on it. Long runs would be better if we had the director there, if contractually they had to come in once every two weeks. There ought to be an Equity contract, saying the theatre director has to see the play once every two weeks, and give notes.

MG: The stage manager fills in.

GAMBON: They don't know. What can they do?

MG: Zero Mostel had a reputation for improvising during a long run. I suppose as much as anything it was to keep himself interested in the role.

GAMBON: Well, I think I've done that. I have behaved badly in the theatre in various plays I've been in. I've been shouted at.

MG: Shouted at?

GAMBON: Yes.

MG: By the audience?

GAMBON: No. By the other actors or by the director – for simply fooling about. I've done some terrible things. I remember one day when we were doing a matinee of *Uncle Vanya* in the West End. [He played Vanya, Jonathan Pryce was Astrov, Greta Scacchi was Yelena in a production directed by Michael Blakemore.] We had been on for six months. We were around the bend with boredom. You can't do *Uncle Vanya* eight times a week for six months and remain sane. One Wednesday, we came on, and the audience was thin. There were about 20 people out there. And there was a man sitting in the front row, and he had propped up an oil canvas against the stage – and he was painting a portrait of Greta Scacchi. And it drove us crazy. I wanted to kill him. He wasn't even watching the play. It just came over me, like a mad feeling. I couldn't control myself. At one point, Uncle Vanya goes berserk. He almost has a fit, he goes wild. I ran around the stage. I picked up the samovar, which was full of water, a couple of gallons. Weighed a ton. I managed to take the lid off the top of it. I ran around the stage with the samovar – Vanya could do that – and at the right moment I engineered a trip, to look like Vanya tripped, and I aimed the samovar at the man doing the painting. It hit him straight in the centre. He was drenched. His oil painting was destroyed. Having done it, then you panic. This is going to be the end of my career. I'm going to be sacked. How could I do this? I turned my back and went upstage, trying to collect myself, to carry on with the scene. I turned around and he was gone. There was no evidence that he had ever been there. I thought, well he's waiting at the stage door, he's going to kill me. He's going to make me pay for all his clothes. It was terrible. The other actors were by that time not speaking to me. At the interval they were appalled, and I was waiting to be beaten up. But he never showed up. And no-one ever mentioned it. That was the worst I've ever done.

MG: Serves him right. The way they announce before a show begins: turn your mobiles off, unwrap your chocolates, and . . .

GAMBON: Do not do oil paintings of the leading lady – particularly on an empty matinee.

MG: You do like to break up actors, to corpse onstage.

GAMBON: I shouldn't mention names, but I'm no worse than Judi Dench. I'm trying to defend myself by mentioning the best actress in the world.

MG: Have you been in a play with her when she did that?

GAMBON: I was in a play with Judi at the Aldwych. Bernard Shaw. She used to corpse a lot. The thing I remember most is that I did a TV play of Ibsen's *Ghosts*, with her as Mrs Alving and Ken Branagh as Oswald. I was Pastor Manders. It was directed by Elijah Moshinsky. And the serving girl was Natasha Richardson. 'Under the opening credits,' he said, 'I want to see all of you sitting around the dark table having dinner.' We said, 'Can we speak – because it's not scripted.' He said, 'Well you can just murmur to each other.' We're all sitting around the table. Even before the shooting started, the table was like that [*jiggling up and down*]. Because Ken is a terrible corpser. And Judi. We were all there. Now Ken has a hand, and she has a hand. We were hanging on for dear life. [*The table begins to rumble, as he recreates the scene.*] Natasha came to me first with a big bowl of potatoes. She said, 'Would you like some potatoes, Pastor Manders?'

MG: Is that in the play?

GAMBON: No! He said we could whisper. So the table started going even more. And I said, 'Yes, please. Can I have twelve?' And they were *enormous* potatoes. And then it went. The whole thing! The director came down onto the floor and said, 'This has got to stop. This is ridiculous.'

MG: Laughing in the night.

GAMBON: I've seen people turning it into crying. So they don't get the sack. Which would be more applicable to the scene.

MG: In *Volpone*, you tried to break up Simon Russell Beale.

GAMBON: Well, only because he didn't have the moral courage to resist it. I broke him up once or twice. I used to break everyone up in that play. There's a long scene in *Volpone*, where the manager has just arrived in town. The salesman speaks Latin. He does a long speech to the townspeople. I just didn't bother about that. I spoke in an Italiana accent. Frank Sinatra. Bob Hope. All these words came into Jonson's Volpone. You could see the audience going, what? It's quite legitimate. The director didn't mind.

MG: Jonson might have minded.

GAMBON: I'm sure he wouldn't have minded. What Volpone is saying there, the audience doesn't understand anyway. So I got most of the American movie stars in there, all sorts of stuff. I used to sing, 'I did it my way,' all in an Italian accent. So I enriched the scene with this funny comedy, which worked for the scene. Simon would agree, I think. The end is much more difficult to do than the beginning, because Volpone doesn't seem at the end to be the man he was at the beginning. It gets rather serious.

MG: You don't like acting in the round.

GAMBON: It seems to me to be wrong. If I'm doing a scene with you in the round and I'm looking at you, on each side of your head I can see a pair of training shoes in the audience. There has to be an area on the stage where the actor has safety. There has to be an area where the audience can't see you, where you can hide from them. There has to be a part in the play where you can play a whole scene with your back to the audience – and express just as much, by the shape of your head, by the way your shoulders hang, by the way your legs move – by the way your whole body expresses something. In theatre-in-the-round, you can't do that.

MG: The first actor I saw who acted with his back to the audience was Olivier.

GAMBON: He loved that. Very powerful.

MG: But with your back to the audience, you can't use your facial features.

GAMBON: But it tells you everything. I used to do it in *A Number* at the end. I think it's very important. Theatre-in-the-round takes that power away from you. I think it was invented by Stephen Joseph in order to travel around schools, which is quite legitimate. You get a group of actors and you get the children to put the chairs in a circle and the group runs into the middle and does their plays. Just like that, quickly. But I think to formalise it – Alan [Ayckbourn, who runs the theatre-in-the-round in Scarborough] will hate me to say this.

MG: At the Swan at Stratford, the stage is three-sided.

GAMBON: Three's OK. You still have to have your area. And with four, you can't have a set. You can't have walls, doors. Maybe you can with a clever design.

MG: In Nigel Hawthorne's autobiography [*Straight Face*], he says that you had 'a wickedly playful streak which very often threatened to make mincemeat of all my theories about being well behaved on matinee days.'

139

GAMBON: Mind you, Nigel can shout. We were in some scrapes together on matinee days. He was just as bad as me. When I acted with Nigel in the West End in *Otherwise Engaged*, his friend John Neville, the great English actor, came to see it, and Nigel was just like a kid because John was coming in. He said, 'You wait to hear him laughing.' It was a thin house again, and we started to play – and it's a very funny play. You could hear John Neville laughing like a hyena. As long as all that doesn't spoil the audience's enjoyment.

MG: A problem might arise if you're doing *Oedipus* or *Long Day's Journey into Night*.

GAMBON: Well, you wouldn't do it then. You couldn't. You wouldn't do it in *A Number*. And you couldn't fool around in *Skylight*. You don't do it if it spoils the play.

MG: Tell me about *Juno and the Paycock* in Dublin. That was not a good experience.

GAMBON: No. It was a mess, really. But I always wanted to play that part [Joxer Daly]. I will do it again one day. I'll do it properly. It's a shame that it was an unfocused production – sloppy. I don't know whose fault it was. People seemed to like it; they came to see it.

MG: You can tell if it's not working?

GAMBON: You feel as if the ship is not floating properly: this isn't working. He shouldn't be there, I shouldn't be here, she shouldn't be there, this is wrong.

MG: That sounds almost as if you're acting as the director.

GAMBON: Well, you have to. I think you have to be aware of what's going on around you.

MG: There are actors who like to upstage other actors.

GAMBON: Yes, that's why we need strong directors – to control them. We wouldn't be on the stage if we didn't want to be seen. But we have to be controlled.

MG: You've got to work with the other actors.

GAMBON: And the better they are, the better it is for you. If they're better actors than you, you're safe. I remember going to Stratford to see *Richard III*. An actor came on, and he only had a couple of lines. I'll never forget it. He stood at the back. He said his lines, and you couldn't take your eye off him. In the interval I looked in the programme. It was Ian Richardson. What an actor! I learned a lesson watching that. Apart from the fact that he came on beautifully, he spoke clearly. There was something about him.

MG: Ayckbourn says in his book that in his production of *A View from the Bridge*, 'I rarely laughed as much in the rehearsal room as I did during the early rehearsals.' That was in direct contrast to *A Small Family Business*, a comedy. In rehearsal, that was played very seriously.

GAMBON: We played *A View from the Bridge* very fast.

MG: And at least during rehearsal there was a lot of laughter – in a very serious play.

GAMBON: That's right. That's usually the case with very serious plays.

MG: Is this then a comment on playing comedy and tragedy?

GAMBON: If you do a comedy and you spend all your time in rehearsal laughing at it, I think it's disastrous. You have to rehearse a comedy absolutely straight. And it's a very serious business. Alan's plays are mathematically worked out. He knows exactly where the laughs are going to come. They're very tight ships to be on, whereas with a drama like *A View from the Bridge*, you can do much more with it. When you rehearse a play as serious as that, you can't help but have fun. Which actually informs the play when you come to do it for real.

MG: Although when you do it for real, there's not much comedy in it.

GAMBON: No. With Alan, we would spend a day rehearsing and then at four o'clock, he would say, 'Let's do a run-through.' And the run-through would be great, because we would suddenly shake off all the fooling around and laughing and do it properly. And the laughing helps.

MG: Ayckbourn also said that some actors think the only way to get laughs is with all the lights on at full. Not true?

GAMBON: No, that's the old-fashioned Olivier theory of laughter: you have to put the lights right up. The audience can see you. 'How am I going to get laughs if the audience can't see me?' That's not true. I can understand why he thinks that. But Alan doesn't worry about that. Good for him.

MG: Recently there was a revival of Albee's *All Over* in New York, starring Rosemary Harris and Michael Learned. Myra Carter, who had starred in *Three Tall Women*, had a tiny role as The Nurse, but she practically walked away with the show: she was very funny. I said to Albee later that Myra was so funny, and he said, 'That's because she thinks the play is about The Nurse.' Sometime later I mentioned that to an actor and he said that he had a friend who was playing the doctor in *A Streetcar Named Desire*, and someone asked him what *Streetcar* was about and he said, 'It's about this doctor who takes this crazy lady off to an asylum.' Then I told both stories to Marian Seldes and she said that the original of the story was when someone asked the actor playing the Gravedigger in *Hamlet* what *Hamlet* was about. Does this mean that the actor playing a small part has to feel that there's something important about his role, if it's not the centre at least it has an importance?

GAMBON: Yes. Absolutely. There's an exercise I once did with a director where there was a hat with numbers in it. You all put your hand in and whatever number you take out, that's how you play the scene. So if you take out number one, you play that in the scene. It's knowing where your levels are, what your status is and how you play your part. When you read a scene and rehearse a scene, you should know your number. You should know you're not number one, you're not number three, you're number eight. Your number can change during a scene. You can go from two to four and then back up.

MG: But if you're playing a small part, you should feel that you're essential to the play.

GAMBON: Absolutely. But not all small parts. The guys at the back with their spears in *Hamlet* are not part of the scene at all. They're just standing there.

MG: Before when we were talking about Prince Charles, you actually used the word 'Macbeth'. You didn't say 'the Scottish play.' You don't believe in the superstition?

GAMBON: I do. In fact, as I said it, I thought I shouldn't have said that. But I usually apply that to dressing rooms, as opposed to a restaurant.

MG: You've done *Macbeth*. I missed it.

GAMBON: You would. It was years ago – in rep. It was not very good. I didn't know what I was doing. I was thirty years old. I was dressed as a spaceman. The concept was that we were in space and so we were all dressed in NASA boiler suits and we almost had helmets. It was terrible. At the dress rehearsal I started walking like I was on the moon. And the director shouted at me, 'Stop fucking it up.' I said, 'But I have this costume.'

MG: When Anthony Hopkins asked you for advice on how to play Lear, what did you say?

GAMBON: I guess Tony was fearful about the Fool. It's an old theatrical story, isn't it? You watch your Fool. Tony Sher, who I saw yesterday, was my Fool, and he made a big perform-ance. A red nose, and I had my hand up the back of his coat, making him a ventriloquist's dummy. The Fool had a very important part, and I suppose Lear could lose out over that.

MG: And Gielgud's advice about playing Lear was to choose a light Cordelia.

143

GAMBON: I didn't have a light one. Choose a light Cordelia, or if you don't have that, get a ladder in the wings. A stepladder. You don't pick her up. You stand like that. And just before you go on, she drops into your arms. These are all practical hints for actors.

MG: Let's move on to your movies and television: *Sleepy Hollow*, *The Insider*, *Path to War.* You've played quite a few Americans.

GAMBON: I got so frightened with the last American I played, Lyndon Johnson [in *Path to War*]. I didn't like my accent. It upset me. I hate all that. You feel you can't play the man because you're worried about the accent. It's like a barrier. You come to do a scene with Alec Baldwin and Donald Sutherland. Quiet in this room! You're worried about this accent – and not about playing Lyndon Johnson.

MG: You have done accents.

GAMBON: Somehow that was harder for me because it was West Texas, and I was frightened how famous he was. It seems to have been successful. But accents bother me. I did a western recently with Kevin Costner, *Open Range*. I play the baddie. I said to him, 'I'm not going to do an American accent. I'm frightened. Let me do it Irish.' He said, 'OK.' There must have been Irishmen in the west. In *The Insider*, I only had two little scenes with Russell Crowe. And so the accent wasn't such a big deal, and it was easier to accomplish that, whereas in Lyndon Johnson, you've got a script that thick. I've got to play this whole part. It's best to do a cameo part in an American movie if you're playing an American. Say four scenes, twelve pages of dialogue – you can cope with it. Because you can hold it in your hand, and say, 'That's what I've got.' And I can manage it, but I can't manage that. I wouldn't have said that to [John] Frankenheimer before we started.

MG: With the *Inspector Maigret* series on television, you just did that straight, without attempting an accent.

GAMBON: Yes. If you did a cod French accent, it would be funny, it would be Inspector Clouseau.

MG: In *Gosford Park*, you had a good role. That was fun, wasn't it?

GAMBON: That was like being on holiday, making that film. All the actors knew each other, all had worked together before.

MG: But you hadn't worked with the director [Robert Altman] before.

GAMBON: Not with the director. And what a director! He's the best; he's full of fun and jokes and games. When we weren't called, we would all turn up anyway. And have lunch on the caterers. We loved it.

MG: You were killed early in the film.

GAMBON: I was killed halfway through. It was upsetting. We used to ask Altman who had the lead and he would say, I can't tell you. It was great. It was a good part, that. A bit of a bastard! But he was working-class money. He wasn't of the manner born, was he? He insinuated his way into their life.

MG: How do you play someone as bad as that?

GAMBON: Easier than playing good people. Good people are boring. And I loved the way he treats people. When Tom Hollander [who plays Gambon's son-in-law in the film] is trying to get me to help him set up a business, I just ignore him. I find that very funny. It made me laugh.

MG: You had to carry that dog in the movie.

GAMBON: I didn't read the script, so I didn't know about that dog. On the first day when Altman came up to me and said, 'Mike, here's your dog,' I didn't want to admit that I didn't know about the dog, so I said, oh, right. And he gave me this dog. So I just held it. I was stuck with it.

MG: You don't like dogs?

GAMBON: I do like dogs, but this dog smelled. I like big dogs. I don't like those yappy dogs. But I love being with Altman. I love watching him directing. I love the way sometimes he has three cameras running on tracks. You do a very complicated scene with ten people in it, and by lunchtime he's done it. That's it. With some directors, you spend two days on that, doing cut-ins and close-ups. He's got this whole thing, moving.

MG: He lets actors create things.

GAMBON: He gives you freedom to do things you want to do. You can improvise in front of the camera. I used to make up lines on a take, and he'd use them. I love that freedom.

MG: And you seldom find that in movies?

GAMBON: Seldom find it. That's the secret of good movie acting, isn't it, to be free in front of the camera, to feel as though you're not trapped, to be free to do what you want to do.

MG: You find a freedom acting onstage. But you don't always find that in films.

GAMBON: No, but I daresay movie stars do find it, which is why they're movie stars. They stand in front of a camera and have that calm relaxation and the confidence, instead of being frightened in front of the camera. An American film actor might say a line twenty times. The camera is just running. He knows there are the scissors. We're much more text-bound and more caught up in scene building, whereas some American actors I've watched are much freer. I'm not too bad now in front of a camera. I can cope with it, but it takes a long time.

MG: You seem to have had a greater career on television than in films.

GAMBON: Well, there's no film industry here really. The television for me dried up for years and then out of the blue four years ago I did a series for BBC, *Wives and Daughters*, and got a BAFTA Best Actor. The next year *Longitude*, I got a BAFTA Best Actor. The next year I did *Perfect Strangers*, got a BAFTA Best Actor. I got three years running three big TV shows. I couldn't believe it. I thought TV for me had finished – it's all for actors under thirty – and suddenly I had all this. Poof! I thought *The Singing Detective* was a fluke, the last award I would ever win. Then all these years later I got the three of them.

MG: Each one is a long series.

GAMBON: They're journeys. Much better for acting, much more layered, more opportunity to show different facets of the character. I couldn't be in a show that had no ending. I don't know how you could play a part that doesn't have an end. Like guys in soaps do that. It has to be a complete journey, where I'm going to, where I'm going to stop, how I'm going to get there.

MG: Your film of *Endgame* was a good experience?

GAMBON: I loved that. When we were rehearsing it – Conor [McPherson, who directed it] is a very amusing man – it's a comedy. It's extremely funny. I'm sure Beckett wrote it to be funny.

MG: Often when it's performed, it can seem weighty.

GAMBON: That's because of the desolation out the window.

MG: Did you add anything to the play?

GAMBON: No. Oh, no! It's like a Bible. It wouldn't feel right. You couldn't add anything to Harold [Pinter] either, could you? It's too brilliant. It would be an appalling thing. When I go near him, I go quiet because I feel I'm in the presence of someone who really knows.

MG: You felt that way with Olivier and those other actors.

GAMBON: Yes. Maybe I'm impressed by authoritarian figures, people who are cleverer than oneself.

MG: People who you *think* are cleverer than yourself.

GAMBON: That's right. It's working-class subservience. Can't get rid of it. Particularly in this country, it's deeply ingrained.

MG: Do you find that you use your knighthood?

GAMBON: No, never.

MG: You don't book a table for Sir Michael?

GAMBON: I'd be embarrassed.

MG: Apparently McKellen uses his knighthood.

GAMBON: Does he? Aaahhh! Well, I heard a story the other day that Ben Kingsley complained on a film set that they weren't calling him Sir Ben. In America, it works well. When I did *The Insider*, they used to call me Sir Gambon. 'Out of your trailer: Sir Gambon.' I think [John] Frankenheimer was impressed by it. I thought that Lyndon Johnson would be more of an event. If you're an actor, you think of events that might change your life. I thought maybe this would help me get work in America.

MG: On the other hand, were there events that you didn't think would change your life that did?

GAMBON: I know I got lots of offers to work from *The Insider*, which was a quick two days. The things you never imagine will help do help.

MG: That was an outrageous character – Tom Driberg – that you played in *Tom and Clem*.

GAMBON: True story, or sort of true. I actually met him in the '60s. Outrageous. Good Labour Party politician. Went to the House of Lords before he died: he became Lord Driberg. The play didn't actually happen. He didn't behave like that with a Russian officer, but it was all the sort of thing he did. He used to smuggle sailors into the House of Commons. But it was a nice play, wasn't it? Nice scene with Alec McCowen [as Clement Attlee].

MG: That was the play that this actor [Stephen Churchett] just submitted blind, and it was picked right up.

GAMBON: Stephen Churchett presented this play to Michael Codron, and Michael rang him up. Stephen couldn't believe it. It happened to be on top of Michael's pile in the morning.

MG: Do you read plays that come to you?

GAMBON: I do. Mainly film scripts come to me. Usually they have no start date. In other words, they're not green-lit. They send you a script and if you say you like it, they put your name on it if they're trying to get the money. They get a list of twenty people who like the script. You think it's been sent to you for a part. I did another film not long ago, *The Actors*, with Conor McPherson, and Michael Caine, a comedy, in Dublin. Written by Conor. A farce, a crazy story about a theatre actor in Dublin, played by Michael Caine. That was terrific fun. I'm doing a little part with Gwyneth Paltrow, in *Sylvia*, the story of Sylvia Plath and Ted Hughes. Then there's another film that's not certain. Apart from that, I'm just pissing around, wondering what's next.

MG: That's the actor's life – wondering what's next.

GAMBON: Yes. When you're not acting, you don't function. You don't know who you are. It definitely affects your state of mind, your happiness.

MG: When *A Number* closed, you felt relief that it was over.

GAMBON: Yeah, but then despair.

MG: Like you'll never work again.

GAMBON: Like you'll never work again. Like you're going to miss Daniel [Craig]. You do work again, but there's a certain emptiness. You lose your function. You're not going out to the theatre every night. Your reason goes.

MG: Playwrights can write plays, painters can paint pictures, but an actor is . . .

GAMBON: He's trapped, because he needs a writer, a director, a theatre, a building, half a million pounds, costumes, wigs, make-up. He's totally dependent on everyone else. He's the victim of the whole system. All he wants to do is stand there and show off. Look at me! He can't, because he needs all this money, and all this whole panoply of English theatre or New York theatre. And a film actor is even worse. A film actor needs $45 million.

MG: How do you stand it?

GAMBON: I've been doing it so long, it's part of me. I think I was born to be an actor. I think it's what I was made to be. I'm sure it was. I think it helps that I'm Irish and it helps that I'm a dreamer – Celtic twilight, and all that. Acting is very sophisticated lying, isn't it? Highly skilled lying.

MG: So highly skilled that we don't know that you're lying.

GAMBON: Yes. You have to believe it. That's the job, to make people believe it. It's got to be. You can't fudge it. I never thought I would do this well, though. I thought it would eventually come to an end: wouldn't last forever. It would stop, and I would do something else. Like a blink of an eye, you wake up after forty years and think, I've done this all my life. I've earned a living, I've got a knighthood. This is remarkable, isn't it? I have a great big country house. I have a Mercedes, a Ferrari; I have forty suits, handmade shoes; I have antiques. And I can pinch myself and think, it's all from being an actor. And I never thought when I started being a professional actor that it would last. I thought it was a phase you go through.

MG: Well, so many actors fall by the wayside.

GAMBON: They give it up. Absolutely. I suppose the secret is not to be a standard type. Be a bit unusual.

MG: Simon Russell Beale said that he felt sorry for beautiful-looking actors because they were limited in what roles they could do.

GAMBON: Absolutely.

MG: There is of course a limit: he can't play handsome leading men.

GAMBON: In the theatre there is no limit: you can get away with it. You can wear wigs, make-up, all sorts of stuff. You can't do that in the movies. Also, you have more of a choice of range of parts if you're an odd type.

MG: You have two cars, a Ferrari and a Mercedes.

GAMBON: Yeah. The Ferrari is a real poseur's car. It's a big powerful V8, bright red, with enormous wheels. It's very basic. No power steering. Big, chunky gearbox, heavy clutch. It's a nightmare to drive, but it's a real car. It's not a pampered car. It bites you back. If you mishandle it, it'll kill you. You can't drive it half-heartedly. You can't hold one hand on the steering wheel. It'll jump out of your hand. You always have to hold the car. Wherever you point it, it goes. It'll skid. It's a relentless driving machine.

MG: Ayckbourn once said that working with you was like driving a Lamborghini: 'You get a bit of open road and put your foot down on their emotional pedal, and you realise the harder you put your foot down, the more they'll give you.'

GAMBON: Once you know your lines and you understand the character [in *A View from the Bridge*] – I understood the character like that [*snaps his fingers*]. The niece, the despair. Once you know those things and Ayckbourn's cleared the way, you just go [*snaps his fingers again*]. I got to like Lyndon Johnson. The more I read about him, the more I read books about him, I wished I'd met him.

MG: I have a feeling that you like your characters, whether we're talking about Davies in *The Caretaker* or Lyndon Johnson.

GAMBON: I like Davies because he's such a fucking bastard. Devious, designing snake – the most untrustworthy animal. He's an untrustworthy devious snake of a man.

MG: And that's why you like him?

GAMBON: Yeah. I love it. Salter [in *A Number*] is a bit boring. There's not a lot to grab hold of in terms of what you can do with it.

MG: I assume that he wants to live the whole thing again and do it right this time.

GAMBON: Absolutely.

MG: But why doesn't he just get married again and have another child?

GAMBON: Well, that wouldn't fit the play. It's not a realistic play. It's a play of ideas, and I suppose that's what it's about. It's a bit hard to accept the fact that he ill-treats the child before, gets rid of him, has one cloned. Given that, you have to do things with it.

But I liked the sound of Lyndon Johnson. I liked to listen to the Oval Office tapes when he was ringing up his tailor in Chicago, wanting to have some new pants made, saying, 'These pants cut my nuts.' Also, he said, 'In these pants, there's not enough room for my money. Every time I sit on the sofa, the money comes out of the pocket and goes down the back of the cushion.' He says that to the tailor in Chicago. He says, 'On the five pairs of pants I want you to make, I want more room for my nuts and deeper pockets for my money. And also my knife. My knife keeps coming out.' He said, 'How can I keep a knife in the pants?' That's amazing. The President of the United States wants to carry loose change in his pocket.

MG: George Bush the elder never carried money. Presidents don't carry money.

GAMBON: Johnson has a pocketful of change, and he has a knife – a folding penknife, which he carries around with him. And he has a one-to-one with a tailor in Chicago about these problems. While the Vietnam war is going on . . .

MG: Did you read Robert Caro's books about him?

GAMBON: I did. And I listened to the tape when his wife said there was a junkyard on the highway in Texas near where they used to live. He said, 'Where?' She said, 'Next to Mrs Brown's house.' He rings up the mayor of the town at three o'clock in the morning, wakes him up. He said, 'You've got a junkyard next to Mrs Brown, get rid of that.' This is hands on, isn't it? It's very man to man. I like that. If it hadn't been for the war, he'd have been a great president, wouldn't he? He was deeply impressed by Harvard and Yale men who sat around him, and he just listened to them, McNamara and all those people. It's a sad story. And then as soon as he left, he died – within four years. He was a master of the Senate. Oh, that mind! I saw a bit of film of the last ever public speech he gave, a gathering of women in Texas, when he retired. He's there with a microphone and a lectern, and he's popping glycerine for the heart. He thinks no-one's noticing. And he died two weeks later. I found the whole thing very moving. When I went to Washington for the showing at the French Embassy, I stood out in the lobby and smoked while the film was being shown for three-and-a-quarter hours. Then all the senators and congressmen who were invited to watch it came out and some old guys were crying. Jack Valenti, who I got to know a little bit, was very tearful. I felt very much at one with these people. We started working there just after 9/11. We delayed a week because of that. Flying there to play an American president after that happened made it worse.

MG: In the Mike Nichols film of Tony Kushner's *Angels in America*, you and Simon Callow play angels.

GAMBON: Played a couple of gays, a couple of angels. We had fun. We were there a week. We did it just because it's Mike Nichols and it's a wonderful play, and Al's [Pacino] in it and Meryl's [Streep] in it, and it's in New York. I suppose most of all maybe because it's Mike Nichols. He's a legendary figure.

MG: What did you do in the film?

GAMBON: We get dressed in nightshirts and we have funny hair, funny faces with weird make-up and we stand around the bed with the guy dying of AIDS. They said to us, this moment you turn around and you see the stage coming up hydraulically out of the floor and a staircase going up to heaven. And the two young actors embrace, and start dancing to 'Moon River'. And I watched this. The camera's on us, and I couldn't stop crying. Nice music, and two of the most beautiful young men in the world. And the story of the play, and Tony Kushner, and AIDS.

MG: You're moved as you talk about it.

GAMBON: Yeah. I think I'm very emotional. Maybe I find it easy to cry.

MG: Do you ever feel that way watching a play?

GAMBON: I would if it was something that particularly appealed to me. If Robert De Niro was in a play in the West End, I'd queue all night to see it. Or Al [Pacino].

MG: Would you be so moved as to cry?

GAMBON: Oh, absolutely. I went to see Baryshnikov and Lynn Seymour in the Royal Ballet in Prokofiev's *Romeo and Juliet*. Jesus, that's the greatest theatrical experience I've ever had. In the famous music, where the whole court comes down, I was in the second row. I found it just overwhelming. But I always felt that about ballet.

MG: No words.

GAMBON: Just the movement. I try to do that in acting. I try to move like a dancer. Is that noticeable?

MG: Ayckbourn said you were a 'light actor in a heavy body'.

GAMBON: That's right. I'm very conscious of physical movement on the stage. If I had been born again, I'd want to be in a different shape. I would be a ballet dancer.

MG: Did you ever study dancing?

GAMBON: No. I once had dinner with Kenneth McMillan who was director of the Royal Ballet, and he saw me in a play, *Tales from Hollywood*. He said to me, 'I think you've got the heart of a dancer.' Out of the blue. I said, 'Well, I have.' He said, 'I want you to be in a ballet.' I said, 'Where?' He said, 'The Royal Ballet.' I said, 'When?' He said, 'Whenever. I want you play the Friar in *Romeo and Juliet*' – the ballet I was just talking about. He said, 'You don't have to dance. You come on with a long monk's habit and you have a vial of poison, and at a certain point in the music, you go like that to Romeo, that to Juliet.' I said, 'God, I'd love to do that!' He said, 'Well, you will.' I was so excited. And then two weeks later he died. I could have actually been a Royal Ballet dancer. I would have been a principal at the Royal Ballet!

MG: Once you were onstage, you would have wanted to dance . . .

GAMBON: I would put a few steps in. When the Friar goes like that [*holds out the poison*], I'd have done more. Maybe with the body. I would like to be involved in something where dancing and acting came together, some sort of show where you could do both. Or someone could dance and someone could act. Or some combination of music and dance and drama.

MG: You haven't done a musical yet.

GAMBON: No, I haven't.

MG: Can you sing?

GAMBON: No. I could get away with it. My favourite musicals are by Sondheim, and you can't do that without singing. You have to be a better singer than I am. It would be rather nice to play a choreographer, and during the choreographic scenes, you would see dancers dancing. The choreographer doesn't dance, because he's older.

MG: Do you dance? Like ballroom dancing?

GAMBON: No. I had to dance as Lyndon Johnson. We had a big ballroom out in Pasadena, and John [Frankenheimer] set it up with all the extras. The Inauguration Ball. And so I'm dancing with Ladybird, after I've been elected, and the two of us go out on the floor. When we were shooting it, I did a couple of circles around. When I got round to my two daughters, I grabbed one of them, pulled her in, and she came with me, and I grabbed the other one. So the four of us went into a waltz, and he left that bit in. We just did it, like that. So you get the family going round in circles.

MG: How would you compare Richardson to Olivier?

GAMBON: Richardson could play any part. He could play the ordinary man and he could play the exotic man. He could fit in any mode – although he couldn't play Hamlet. And he couldn't play Romeo. Although he did play 'The Unmentionable' [Macbeth], with disastrous results [directed by Gielgud, in 1952, at Stratford-upon-Avon]. And he ended up having the whole of the company at Stratford looking for his box [not the box that Gambon gave him]. He said, 'You've all got to find my box.' They said, 'What is it?' 'A little box like that. I had it yesterday. It's inlaid with gold. It's made of tortoise shell.' He had fifty actors looking for it, in the dressing rooms, in the wings. Someone finally said to him, 'What is this box? What's in it?' He said, 'My talent.' True story. He was heartbroken.

MG: Without the box?

GAMBON: He felt he lost his talent.

MG: Was it a real box?

GAMBON: No, it was just metaphorical. His talent was gone. 'My talent was in the box. It's lost.'

MG: Where does Guinness fit in? More like Richardson?

GAMBON: Guinness doesn't fit in so readily because he doesn't belong in the theatre. Or he was not so heavily involved in the theatre.

MG: His greater career was in films.

GAMBON: Essentially Guinness is remembered as a film actor, whereas Gielgud and Richardson certainly are remembered as theatre actors.

MG: Though Guinness had some great moments in the theatre.

GAMBON: Absolutely, but they were well before the time that I remember. In my lifetime the three greats were Olivier, Gielgud and Richardson. I saw Guinness doing *Ross* in the West End, about T.E. Lawrence. Which I remember clearly, and that was terrific. Then Michael Bryant took over for him. Michael was a great stage actor and before that he was an English television star in high class TV dramas. He spent 30 years here [at the National]. He had a brass plate on his door.

MG: Brass plate with his name? Do many actors have that?

GAMBON: Not here, they don't. An actor is never here for more than a year. Your contract is for a year. But Michael actually screwed a brass plate on the door. He was the actor member of the Board. He was a permanent fixture here.

MG: That certainly was a career.

GAMBON: Absolutely. It wouldn't work for me. I'd get restless. I wouldn't stay. I have to keep moving.

MG: Bryant would do small parts, big parts.

GAMBON: He would do anything they offered him, within reason, and he enjoyed it. I think he liked the freedom. Ideal for him. He didn't have a personality that dragged him away. He also didn't like the alternatives. The alternatives were mainly crap on television, and small parts in films. So what's the point?

MG: You might say the same thing about Scofield.

GAMBON: Yes, absolutely. I hear that David Suchet has moved to LA. He's just settled over there with his family because he wants a film career. Good luck to him.

MG: Anthony Hopkins is an American citizen now. I don't think we'll see him onstage again.

GAMBON: I think if someone asked him and he had the right part, he would. When Tony says he's never going to act in the theatre, I don't believe that. He wants you to lament it. I'm sure he doesn't believe it.

MG: On the other hand, if and when he came back to the stage, he would be a box-office star.

GAMBON: Oh, yes, absolutely. And it would have to be successful, or he'd go mad. If Tony came back and did a play in London, it would have to be an enormous hit.

MG: Then you have the two Dames [Maggie Smith and Judi Dench] in David Hare's play, *Breath of Life.*

GAMBON: They're all right, because they do it all the time. But for a film actor, it's a much bigger deal. But the two Dames are two old theatre girls, and they're never off the stage, so we don't mind. They have film careers as well. And Judi's won an Oscar. But for an English guy working in England, there's not a lot of scope around.

MG: Would you do another television series?

GAMBON: I would if it was good. I like the idea of classy TV. What I never wanted is popularity.

MG: I'm shocked, shocked.

GAMBON: I can't think of anything worse than being some-one whose face is so well known that people stop you in the street. I think I've achieved being an actor without anyone knowing anything about me. A lot of the television I appear in isn't watched by most people. It's watched by a very small percentage of the audience. *The Singing Detective*, the average Joe didn't watch that.

MG: The reputation of that show was far in excess of the actual audience.

GAMBON: That's right. The audience was quite small. Then it got famous because of the scenes in it and the controversy. The things I've done since then, quite high-class BBC drama, are not watched by vast numbers of people. I quite like that.

MG: But the popularity, the recognition is not something you crave?

GAMBON: No, that's something that frightens me a bit. When you're a kid you just want to be an actor. It's like being a priest or a doctor. It's a calling. That's how I see it. It's like something inside you that you can't stop. I want to be a doctor, I want to be a priest, I want to be an actor. So you never think of the consequence of that. The consequence of that could be that you become very famous. I'm not very famous. I'm quite well known. When you first become an actor, you just want to be an actor, but you don't think of the consequence of it.

MG: But some do court the fame – from Olivier to Kenneth Branagh. Not so much with Gielgud.

GAMBON: I think he was called to be an actor. And that's what he did. He was a working actor. Not long before he died, he was ringing up his agent asking for work. Sweet, touching.

MG: His last performance was in Beckett's *Catastrophe*, with Pinter.

GAMBON: He loved it. I think that's wonderful. He wanted to act.

MG: But in his case, he did become insular and isolated. He wouldn't know that wars were going on.

GAMBON: That's right. That's not very good. You have to take the world on if you're an actor. I like to do all the other stuff. It also helps acting, if you do other things. Some actors only act. They don't do anything else at all. They don't think about anything else. That's fine. But it wouldn't suit me.

MG: There are actors like Robert Morley, who loved playing the same part for long runs.

GAMBON: But he wasn't crying and tearing the wall down. They were light parts. He could do it without much thought. I remember he did an Alan Ayckbourn play and tried to change it all. It didn't suit him. That wouldn't happen now. We don't live that sort of life any more. We're much different people. You're very conscious when you work at the Royal Court that the Royal Court has to do with education. It has education departments and outreach departments and children's departments. The theatre has a political element; it has to do with sociology and education. When you mention show business, they don't like that. I see it essentially as 'show biz'.

MG: You're not an educator.

GAMBON: No, no. That's incidental.

MG: As difficult as it is to be a stage actor in London, it's so much more difficult in New York.

GAMBON: Yeah, I feel sorry for American boys and girls who want to be actors, who want to do theatre. It's impossible. What you have to do is make your own. And they do, in fact. At least here there is an industry that is one hundred years old and runs quite well. In this country, you had a full-time repertory company in every city, with actors earning enough money to bring up their families. And in Germany and France, the same, in every major city. It's a tragedy what's happened. Now we have a handful. Birmingham Rep, maybe, Bristol Old Vic. I knew actors in the '60s who brought up their families, made a living just doing that, going from one rep to another, all over the country. They dream maybe one day of being in a West End play. The old route: you went to drama school, you went to the Birmingham Rep, then you went to the Old Vic, then you became a movie star. That used to be the classic English actor's route – if you were lucky. I went to the Old Vic and then to Birmingham Rep, the other way around. I think all drama students should study engineering. People say it's funny me being a mechanic and an engineer and an actor. I say it's not funny at all. The two are very linked. I think there's a sort of precision and structure about acting. You shouldn't notice it, should you? With Daniel [Craig] in *A Number*, I told him to wear different shoes one day. He was just wearing trainers. He came on in different shoes and he felt much better. He felt grounded. I think a lot of it comes through your feet.

MG: Judi Dench apparently wants to be grounded physically whenever she acts. When she did *A Little Night Music*, she had to sit on a bed and her feet did not reach the ground. Finally she leaned against the headboard and that served as her grounding.

GAMBON: I understand that completely. Actors sometimes carry a penny in their hand – all through *King Lear* or *Antony and Cleopatra* or Chekhov. The audience can't see it. It's a solidity. You can do this and no-one will notice that you are doing it, and even if they did it wouldn't matter. You can hold it.

MG: Have you done that?

GAMBON: I have done that, yes. I did it with a stone in *King Lear*. I had a pebble which I always carry.

MG: I didn't see it.

GAMBON: Oh, no. I've still got it.

MG: Your *Lear* pebble. You could frame it.

GAMBON: It's on a mantelpiece.

MG: What does that do?

GAMBON: I don't know. I can't explain that. A feeling of solidity, that you're holding something. It makes it easier. I think shoes are very important. From them springs the whole feeling in the body. Talk about engineering. Yat Malmgren, the wonderful teacher of movement at the Drama Centre, talked about how you express yourself with your body and how your body sits on the stage and how you present your-self. It's very to do with mechanics, of how your body is hung.

MG: I studied Alexander for a while, and when I did I sat up straight.

GAMBON: Then you forgot. But when you did, you felt quite good. It does change you.

MG: You talk about the importance of shoes.

GAMBON: Oh, I've got hundreds of shoes. I had a pair of shoes once that I stole from the National Theatre. I wore them in a play here. They suited me. I took the shoes from here and I wore them in a movie. They said to me, 'Are you wearing those shoes?' I said, 'Yes, they're my own shoes.' So then I wore them in a play on the West End. I wore them in another film. I wore them in a TV show. I wore them in twelve productions.

MG: Lucky shoes?

GAMBON: This particular pair of shoes – they just felt so good.

MG: What was the first thing you wore them in?

GAMBON: The first thing I wore them in was playing a butler in a farce [directed] by Alan Ayckbourn.

MG: *Tons of Money.* It was hilarious.

GAMBON: They were very straight, English, formal, toe-capped shoes that a butler would wear. But I then wore them playing quite smart people and playing plain people. Comedy, tragedy – same shoes. [*Laughs.*]

MG: Quoting Peggy Ramsay, Ayckbourn said, 'If you believe you have talent, then be generous with it.' The idea is: don't hold on to one concept. That would apply to actors who play one role and are afraid to try anything else. You're absolutely the opposite.

GAMBON: I sometimes think I should be braver, and try to do something really radically different. I did *The Caretaker* and now *A Number*, and those two characters are wildly different, and yet something in me wants to do something unlike I've ever done before. I do have a wide range. I suppose, in your heart it's all the same thing: it's you. But I'd like to do something really different. I can't say what.

MG: Anything in Shakespeare or the Greeks that you have your eye on?

GAMBON: I've got to play Falstaff eventually. Peter [Hall] has asked me several times and Matthew Warchus has asked me, and others, and I suppose I've just avoided it, but I'll do it eventually. That's a wonderful part, but it means committing yourself for quite a long time. I suppose I get a bit worried about that.

MG: Would you do Lear again?

GAMBON: I would, yes.

MG: You were young when you did it.

GAMBON: I was 42. I would do it again. Not happily. But you've got to.

MG: Stratford is not calling?

GAMBON: You can't spend six months of your life up in Stratford. It's a Shakespeare theme park. Ye Olde England, with thatched cottages and tourists. Somehow you want to do plays for a different sort of people.

MG: What about *Skylight* on Broadway?

GAMBON: That was a good, intelligent audience. Some nights the silence was like black velvet. I suppose I've liked playing to the audience you get here in the Cottesloe. They tend to be a bit younger, and a bit more turned on. You have to get something from an audience. They have to give you something, and it encourages you to do your best. If they're indifferent and not with you . . .

MG: You should have another crack at Chekhov.

GAMBON: I would like that. I'd quite like to play Trigorin. That's a good part – in *The Seagull.* I've run out of what I want to do.

MG: I suppose the easiest thing is memorising lines.

GAMBON: Not now. It's hard. It gets harder and harder. Now I find it very difficult. Very frightening. The same with all actors – when you get to a certain age, it becomes increasingly difficult to get them in your head. I had a terrible problem with *The Caretaker.*

MG: Would you ever forget where you were in the play?

GAMBON: If that ever happens to me, I can always get out of it. I keep talking, wiggle around and come back on track. *A Number* was hellish difficult to learn. It is a worry.

MG: What is that classic story about Gielgud and Richardson being onstage – and going blank? The prompter kept giving the line to them, and finally one of them said, 'We know the line. Which one of us says it?'

GAMBON: 'We know the line. We don't know who says it.' Richardson had a terrible time learning lines toward the end of his life. It becomes a nightmare. When we did the Beckett movie [*Endgame*], we had an autocue machine because we didn't get any rehearsal time. Wherever you looked on the set, there was a screen. It was brilliant. Your lines are just scrolling around. You glance here, you glance there, wherever you look. It's like being relieved of an enormous burden. And your acting is helped too because you don't have to think, what am I going to say next? I think we should get them in every theatre. [*Laughs.*] Sometimes in *A Number*, we both did a little trip and left a line out, but we were in control of it.

MG: You might come back to that play?

GAMBON: I think we might. We could do it at a festival somewhere, in Sydney, Toronto, or maybe in Brooklyn – for two weeks. It's an ideal play for that. It has no set. Having said that, I must keep reading it and make sure I don't forget it.

MG: Actors often look for a character they can impersonate and do a one-man show. Tom Courtenay is doing Philip Larkin.

GAMBON: And Simon Callow is doing Dickens. Alec McCowen did the Bible. It's like having an insurance policy.

MG: Does that hold any interest for you?

GAMBON: No. Oh, Jesus, no. I'd forget it instantly.

MG: You wouldn't want to be onstage by yourself?

GAMBON: No, no. The more the better. Six is a nice number.

MG: Having just done two, six is a nice number?

GAMBON: I did two with Eileen [Atkins in *The Unexpected Man*], three with *The Caretaker*. I think it was five with *Tom and Clem*. But about fifty with *Cressida*. That was great fun. A big family.

MG: With Ayckbourn, it's often six characters.

GAMBON: That's his standard number – three men, three women.

MG: You did *Art* on radio, with Alan Bates and Simon Russell Beale. It's a play about a painting. How do you do that on radio?

GAMBON: It was so bad doing it. When Simon was speaking, Alan and I went [*makes a face*]. When I'm speaking, Simon and Alan. It's so funny that play, if you all know each other, the three actors. We could never do that play on the stage, we three. It would be appalling – because Bates would never stop laughing. And even Russell Beale would start laughing.

MG: But why do it on radio?

GAMBON: I don't know. We just did *A Number* on radio last week. Work that out. You don't see the physical relationship. We had to cut the crying out; it was confusing. God knows. You don't see any smoke rising.

'He made me do one scene 32 times – 32 takes. I didn't know what he was after and he wouldn't tell me . . . I thought maybe he thinks I find acting too easy, and he's going to make me find it difficult'

A little before 12.30 I was back at the National and found Gambon smoking and reading the Evening Standard. *Again he was in a blue business suit and tie – and, I noticed, he was wearing red socks: a devilish touch. The Terrace restaurant was closed, so we brought coffee back to the smoking area and settled in for a long conversation. He began by asking me about the terrorist attack on the World Trade Center in 2001, and he told me where he was that day.*

GAMBON: It was about two o'clock. It was quite a cold day. I sat in a café outside on the pavement and had a cup of coffee. All of a sudden, there was a horn, and I looked over and there's a brand new Bentley Azure, quarter of a million English pounds, driven by Mel Smith, English comedian-actor. I know him. He sold his television company called Talkback Productions for £65 million. He and Griff Rhys-Jones. He was sitting in the car. He said, 'Come and have a drive. My new toy.' He had the radio on, and that's when it happened. I remember saying to him, 'Oh that's a twin-engine Aztec. Some idiot has just clipped the corner of the building.' They carried on, how it was on fire. I couldn't work out how it could be on fire. And then of course I got home, and everyone in this country shut down. I'll never forget it. And then the fourth plane going down in Pennsylvania. And then the phone started ringing. As it unfolded, I was looking at the TV set. I kept thinking there were 20,000 people in that building. If the plane had hit the building three hours later, and lower, it would have wiped out . . .

MG: And to see those people leap out of windows.

GAMBON: I remember having dinner in that restaurant in the World Trade Center. Top of the World.

MG: For me, there was one strange comic sidelight to a horrendous day. As we were watching the attack on television, the telephone rang. It was the copy desk at the *New York Times* saying, 'About your piece on Oscar Wilde, which is running in tomorrow's paper . . . '

GAMBON: It's not going to run?

MG: 'It *is* going to run, and we have a few questions.' I had written about an exhibition of Oscar Wilde opening at the Morgan Library. And it ran the next day in the arts section, with large pictures, in an issue otherwise devoted to the terrorist attack.

GAMBON: It's ridiculous, isn't it?

MG: I thought later, Oscar would have liked that.

GAMBON: He would have loved that.

MG: When you were on Broadway in *Skylight*, did you make contact with any gunsmiths?

167

GAMBON: I tried to, but I felt cut off. Golden opportunity missed. I asked a policeman one day sitting in a café – that's how sad I was – I said, 'Do you know any antique gun collectors in New York?' He said, 'I beg your pardon.' I said, 'Antique guns. I like them. 18th-century.' He said, 'They can't have them in New York. They're not allowed to.' Since then, I found out that's not true. There are lots of rich people on Park Avenue with big collections. So I missed all that. I'll rectify it next time.

MG: You haven't yet done a tour in America.

GAMBON: No. I'd like to see America. I could make contact with all these geeks. An actor friend of mine goes over to America and gives lecture tours in engineering. He talks to all these societies and clubs in all these small towns where these guys live – about 19th-century techniques.

MG: You could do that.

GAMBON: I could do it, yes.

MG: I noticed in the National Theatre bookstore that there are books in which Vanessa Redgrave, Corin Redgrave and others each talk about one role. You could do one on acting, on Galileo or Lear, and you could also do one on . . .

GAMBON: Machine tools and airplanes. I know a group in Toronto that collects English firearms. They asked me to go over and give a talk on restoration techniques. I think I'll do that.

MG: Do you still fly planes?

GAMBON: I let that slip. I'll start again one day. My interest in all that is cyclical. I turn on to something else. The only constant is acting. My other pursuits go up and down, depending on my state of mind. Now I'm heavily into the re-creation of a pre-computer precision workshop. Toolroom, they call it. We're talking about late '50s, early '60s. I'm half-way there. It will be like a museum, like a tribute to European and American manufacturing, pre-computers.

MG: And you'll have guided tours, as in those stately homes?

GAMBON: No-one will be allowed in there. I'll be the only one. It will have examples of all the most famous machine tools made mainly in Germany and Switzerland and America, pre-computer. I've got half of them already.

MG: What sort of things can you do with them?

GAMBON: You can do anything you like.

MG: Like build a house, repair a car?

GAMBON: They're higher class than that. You could make a watch, you could make a highly complicated piece of equipment. I find them very beautiful things. That's my particular passion, but when these passions start up in me, then I get worried that I'm going off acting a bit. So I have to keep it in check. I'm at a low point. I finished the play and I'm about to start a little part in a movie, and there might be one in January, and I'm feeling a bit low about acting.

MG: You're out of work right now?

GAMBON: I've got nothing to hang on to. Nothing is really turning me on, so these other pursuits come in my head and start taking me over.

MG: If someone went back and asked your schoolteachers if you acted, they wouldn't . . .

GAMBON: . . . even remember. They wouldn't even know.

MG: They would remember you for your interest in engineering.

GAMBON: Or that I spent most days dreaming, staring out the window. I was just hopeless, always pretending to be some-one else, now that I look back on it. I used to walk around the streets with an empty banjo case. I remember that. So that people thought I played the banjo. It's true.

MG: But you didn't learn the banjo.

GAMBON: No, I didn't have a banjo. But I found an empty banjo case. I shouldn't be telling you all this. [In an earlier conversation, he said that he played the banjo.] My best friend was an Indian boy who lived nearby, we used to spend most of our time together just telling lies to each other. We would know they were lies. We would talk all day to each other while we were fishing. We used to fish in the Regent's Park canal, just near the zoo. We'd fish there on Saturday mornings, for small gudgeon. Then we'd break into the zoo through a hole in the fence, and spend the afternoon there. I love the zoo. I still go.

MG: Reminds me of the movie, *Turtle Diary*.

GAMBON: That's right. I did *Turtle Diary* in that zoo. And we'd take the fish we caught in the morning and then sell them in the afternoon, after the zoo, to the fish shop down in Parkway in Camden Town as bait. They bought live gudgeon as bait. That was my childhood, really.

MG: You say now that you like people to suggest roles to you, but clearly the decision to be an actor was all yours.

GAMBON: It wasn't an important decision. I didn't think of it as important. It was just what I did.

MG: And if it didn't work out?

GAMBON: I'd do something else. No big deal. Nowadays people don't think like that, because the world is different. But when I was a kid, you'd pick up the evening paper in London – there were three evening papers – and the job sections were that thick. No question of never having a job, or not earning money.

MG: But you would have worked with your hands.

GAMBON: I would, which I love. I still do. So unemployment didn't really exist. It was no big decision.

MG: What did you parents say?

GAMBON: Nothing. I didn't even think about it. The first time my dad saw my acting was when I went to Birmingham Rep. I played Othello when I was 27, blacked up as Othello. He and my mum drove up to Birmingham to a matinee. It must have been a terrible shock. I said to them on the phone before they came up, you come round back and see me after the performance. I had another one in the evening so I left all the black make-up on, all the costumes and jewels hanging off me. Then my mum and dad came round to the backstage. They couldn't speak. My dad just was staring. I must have looked like a madman. My mum said she liked it, and nothing much else was said. They were both in shock. And then they went.

MG: Your career just evolved.

GAMBON: I wake up now and I think it all happened so quickly, and I think, oh, shit. I wish I had it all again.

MG: Along the way, you did eight or nine Ayckbourns.

GAMBON: Including some of the plays Alan writes which are three plays and *Sisterly Feelings*, which is two plays depending on which way a coin turns out – I think I've done about twelve Ayckbourn plays. My favourite play of Alan's was the one I did at Scarborough when I did *Othello*. [It was a revival of *Taking Steps*.] I've seen and read *Relatively Speaking*, which is one of Alan's earliest plays. I think that's hilarious. I'd like to do that. On TV I've done the one about the woman who's trying to kill herself in the kitchen. *Absurd Person Singular*. He's written some very funny stuff. I don't see Alan anymore. I suppose after *Othello* and the season I did up there – that wasn't a terrifically happy experience. I should renew my acquaintance with him.

I had a letter from Alec Guinness when I did *Man of the Moment*. He was very flattering. He said he had come to see the show and my performance renewed his interest in acting. That was a thrill. Renewed his interest in acting. Then he came to see me in the Yasmina Reza play [*The Unexpected*

171

Man] in the West End. I knew he was in because he's a friend of Eileen Atkins. She said, he's coming round afterwards. I thought, oh god, I'm really looking forward to it. And he came round – and he didn't speak to me. He just said, hello, and that was it. I thought of the letter he wrote me, and I thought he'd be my friend. He hardly looked at me when he came back.

MG: What do you do when you go round to an actor's dressing room after a performance, and you haven't liked what you've seen?

GAMBON: Just tell lies. If you see a play and your friend's in it, you can't go round and say to your friend, 'I thought you were terrible.' So I go round and say, 'I thought you were brilliant.' Part of you does think that, because he's your friend.

MG: You wouldn't say something ambiguous, like 'That really was something'?

GAMBON: I wouldn't be able to do that. Once I had a friend who played Othello at the Mermaid. He wasn't terrific. He was too young for Othello. We went out and had something to eat. I told him how brilliant he was, but a couple of hours later I was drunk, I started picking holes. I said, when you say that, you shouldn't do this, when you come out to do this, you shouldn't do that.

MG: Dustin Hoffman is a friend and when I would see one of his plays, he would say to me, 'What didn't you like about it?'

GAMBON: I can understand that, because the compliments just become all one. You can learn more from people telling you what you shouldn't be doing.

MG: To get back to Ayckbourn, you've played so many of his characters.

GAMBON: But it's over some time, and I tend to play the

172

same sort of character in Ayckbourn plays – the dummy character, which I like best. The guy hasn't got a brain. They're much more fun to play. *Man of the Moment* is one of those guys. And the vet in *The Norman Conquests*. He doesn't know what's going on. I find them very appealing, whereas in *A Small Family Business*, I played the guy who's running the business. He's quite wary, and he turns into a Mafia boss, and that was good fun. Sometimes you can drive one of Alan's plays like that. You can be the driver, but other people get the laughs. It's usually the dummy that gets more laughs. In *Man of the Moment*, Samantha Bond drove the play. She didn't get many laughs at all. She was frustrated by that.

I really like Simon Russell Beale. He's a different generation to me, and so I want him so much to be the great actor. But if he was my age. [*Laughs.*] . . . I dunno, I wouldn't be so generous, I suppose. But for Simon who's twenty years younger than me, I follow him with eyes wide open.

MG: People have said that each of you is the actor of his generation.

GAMBON: Well, well, I don't know. I haven't seen him in that double bill [*Uncle Vanya* and *Twelfth Night*, directed by Sam Mendes].

MG: He's extraordinary.

GAMBON: And now that you're talking about him, I'm beginning to hate him again.

MG: Younger though he is.

GAMBON: Younger though he is. Bastard. [*He laughs.*]

MG: He wants to play Falstaff. Who's going to get to it first?

GAMBON: Well, I probably won't. He'd better do it. He'll speak it more clearly than I will, and maybe he'll get more sense out of it.

MG: But you would be funnier and more moving in the end.

GAMBON: Maybe. I'd better do it quick. Because he'll jump on that. He wants to do Galileo, so you told me. He's too young for it. So maybe by the time he completely erases the memory of *me,* I'll be too old to worry about it.

MG: Simon Callow just did Galileo on television. Not the Brecht play.

GAMBON: Simon told me about that. He just mentioned it in New York. It made me angry, but I didn't say anything. I pretended to be happy.

Sometimes people propound a theory to me about acting, which is quite correct, and I think, oh, that's it. But I forget it immediately. Else I'd say it now.

MG: Do you know Peter Brook?

GAMBON: I met him. He came to see *King Lear*, and he said to me when I saw him backstage: 'Good work.' That's all he said. I thought that was quite complimentary. 'Good work.' Then he once wanted me to be in a film he was directing, and it didn't work out.

MG: You've worked with Deborah Warner.

GAMBON: I love her. I did a film for her, *Last September*, which we shot in Ireland. I played the dad and Maggie Smith was my wife. The house was filled with young people, and it was well directed. Maybe a bit slow. It never got seen much. But I loved working with Deborah. We had a proper rehearsal time beforehand, and we got to know each other. Six weeks shooting, near Dublin.

MG: Yesterday we were talking about the difference between acting in Olivier's day and acting today. Your feeling seemed to be that it had all changed.

GAMBON: It's all exploded. There are so many actors now. They've doubled, or tripled.

MG: In those days, an actor could make a living just working in the theatre.

GAMBON: Many did. You couldn't do that now. Alan at Scarborough has a permanent company for a year, but that's rare. But then, many actors made their living on the stage. There must be thousands of actors today who don't earn a living as actors. I heard that Peter Hall said once that he could get all the actors and actresses who work with continuous regularity on TV, film and theatre in this country in his apartment. I'm sure that's true. I'm sure ninety per cent of the graduates of drama schools can't hope to make a living as actors.

MG: I would say that you're basically a naturalistic actor.

GAMBON: Yes. I think my generation were able to get the naturalism of the modern American wave. That influenced us tremendously – De Niro, Pacino, Hoffman, John Malkovich. If you're steeped in theatre acting, you take what those guys do, and you mix and match them. I think that's what I've done, unconsciously at times. I appear in a play and give it its theatrical value but also give it that sort of profound realism and lock them together.

MG: You've worked with so many of the top English actresses.

GAMBON: Maggie, Judi, Eileen, then the young ones. I played Julia Roberts's father, Helena Bonham Carter's father. I should be playing their lovers.

MG: You were saying before that Stratford had turned into a theme park. Do you think it's changed since you were there in *Lear* and *Antony and Cleopatra.*

GAMBON: It was in the days before the Swan was built. It wasn't what it's become; it was a much smaller community. I remember Pete Postlethwaite went into a shop in the main street one day because he saw a sign in the shop window, 'Jeans, ten per cent off to the RSC.' Walked in and tried the jeans on, bought them and said, give me my ten per cent, and the guy said, 'I thought you'd be in the Falklands. Why aren't you in Falklands?' RSC meant the Royal Signal Corps which is an English regiment based in Stratford – not the Royal Shakespeare Company. Pete said, 'I'm at the RSC. I'm at the Royal Shakespeare Company.' He said, 'What's that?'

When I went to Stratford it was for almost 18 months. That's too much. You went to Stratford, then you went to Newcastle for a season there, you came back to the Barbican. It was relentless. I've never been back. Too much to commit to. But I enjoyed it. I'm glad I did it. If you're an actor, you have to go to Stratford at some point.

MG: For the audience, it was great to see actors move from role to role.

GAMBON: Thrilling. And to see them get better and better and bigger parts. Look at Ian Holm who started there years ago

MG: I wrote a long article about Mia Farrow when she was at the RSC. She so enjoyed being there.

GAMBON: I was there when she was there. I did a show with her, that orchestral piece by Honegger, *Joan at the Stake* at the Royal Albert Hall, with André Previn conducting. She played Joan, a speaking part, and RSC actors played the other characters.

MG: I remember one of her friends in those days was an actor who was really a comer, and seems to have disappeared: Mike Gwilym.

GAMBON: Ahh, well, Mike Gwilym gave it all up. He got fed up with it, he didn't like it anymore and he went to Spain. He had some money he inherited and he bought a little house. I was talking about him last week. For twenty years he hasn't acted. He just reads, walks on the beach, cooks some food. I think he just hated it.

MG: Have you found other actors who might have had a career and for whatever reason gave it up?

GAMBON: There's a whole group of actors of my generation who used to earn a living on TV and never work now but are still very well known. Michael Jayston. Anthony Valentine. Because of the lack of drama on television, they only do soaps.

MG: In *A Small Family Business*, you injured your ankle.

GAMBON: They left cables in the wings of the stage and on the press night I was running into the wings, and I fell. Over I went. I'll never forget it. I didn't go on for two weeks. The understudy played in front of the critics. I went to hospital. Then I came back and all the critics were invited back to see it – and they thought he was better than me.

The thing I enjoyed here [at the National] was the other one, *A Chorus of Disapproval*, where I played the Welsh theatre director. That was good fun. Bob Peck was in that. It was a big hit and then went to the West End, where Colin Blakely took over. That would have been about 1985. Just between ourselves, Colin got frustrated by that play. He didn't realise that halfway through it gets very serious. His wife goes round the bend and the audience stops laughing. I'd like to see a production of that play, with a radically new director.

MG: Is that a problem when you have the playwright directing his own work?

GAMBON: No, Alan's good for that. He knows it all thoroughly. He knows exactly what he wants. He knows where every laugh is and he knows how to get them. For the sort of playwright Alan is, he's the perfect director for his own work. I wouldn't imagine Caryl Churchill would be much of a director for *A Number*. Harold is a good director. He works very straight. I've worked twice with him. There's no bullshit. There's nothing superfluous. If there's nothing to do, you don't do anything. I like that sort of simplicity. It's like his writing – sparse.

MG: Did you hesitate about bringing *Skylight* to New York?

GAMBON: I was nervous about it. I didn't think the New York audience would latch on to the fact that our social welfare system is different and that the character played by Lia Williams was a teacher and committed to the poor but had this rich man who loved her. I wasn't sure they would get all that, but they did. I did think her character lost out in a way. The man's more alluring, funnier in what he does, what he says. When we were rehearsing in New York, David [Hare] and Richard [Eyre] tried to take some lines out in order to make Lia's character less obtuse, less severe. I complained because it affected my responses to what she said.

When I played Oscar Wilde on television, I did a bit of research about him. He had black teeth because of mercury poisoning. He had hands like me – long hands. Wilde always covered his mouth when he spoke. I tried to shovel a lot of that in it, but the television people wouldn't let me. They said it was too much. I said, 'Do you want the real truth of Oscar Wilde or do you want some silly story?' They said, 'Well, we can't have that on TV. You can't have black teeth.' I said, 'So why are you making the story of Oscar Wilde?' They said, 'Well, it's a good script.' I said, 'But why are you doing it if you don't want to be true.' They said, 'Well, the audience wouldn't like it.' Weird, isn't? Sad man. And then when David Hare wrote the play about him – I'd love to have done that part. Big Liam [Neeson] played him.

I'd love to do a play about him in Paris before he dies. I was reading the other week that some famous French tragedian saw him in the street. She recognised him as Oscar Wilde and said, 'Come to my house tonight for dinner.' He turned up, and she was expecting him to entertain the people. He sat there in silence, had his dinner, drank all the wine, and when he was going he asked her, 'Could you let me have 5000 francs?' She said no. He walked out. That's true. He died two months later.

MG: How do you feel about his plays?

GAMBON: They're not my sort of thing. They're too grand.

MG: *The Importance of Being Earnest* would not be your play.

GAMBON: I would just spend the whole night laughing. I couldn't take it seriously. I could play old Canon Chasuble.

MG: You could play Lady Bracknell.

GAMBON: I would be brilliant as Lady Bracknell. Big wig. We had an Englishman play Lady Bracknell here. He's an excellent actor. I can't remember his name. [Bette Bourne.] I went to see him. I was crying because he's a friend of mine. But I would just cause chaos. Jack Worthing and Algernon Moncrieff would just not be able to play their parts.

MG: Your eyes light up at the thought.

GAMBON: Brilliant.

MG: Have you ever played a woman?

GAMBON: No. I'd like that. I'd be very good as a woman. Have to be a well-established woman. I could play Volumnia in *Coriolanus*. But it would be a comedy.

MG: Tell me about *Dancing at Lughnasa*.

GAMBON: Ahh. Beautiful play. I was the mad priest, the brother, the drug addict. It didn't seem to work. I suppose it's essentially a theatrical experience. The dance is a highlight, and it didn't happen in the film. Friel has asked me to do other plays. He asked me to do the play where the three stand on the stage and talk [*Faith Healer*]. I love his work, but I've never been able to do one. I loved *Translations*. I think all young people should see that play. It's so educational about Ireland.

MG: *Wives and Daughters*.

GAMBON: I won an award for that. I was a nice old fella who turns out to be a good man in the end. A rascally old fucker who comes round to knowing what love is. Happy ending. Good story. Unfinished novel by Mrs Gaskell. It went down well.

MG: You've done well with mini-series. *Longitude* was a challenge.

GAMBON: Yeah. I loved that. That was fascinating. Clocks and machinery. Charles Sturridge did such a good job with that script, and directed it himself. He's a clever man, really brought it together, although I had one or two hard days with him. He made me do one scene thirty-two times – thirty-two takes. I had a speech that long [*hands far apart*], at the end of which I had to cry, which is tough. I suppose that speech might be three minutes of screen time. Thirty-two times!

MG: Each time you cried?

GAMBON: Yep. I wouldn't give up. I didn't know what he was after, and he wouldn't tell me. I could see the producer in the corner of the room looking perplexed. After take five, he went [*a look askance*]. I didn't look at Sturridge. He just kept saying, 'Again.' So I did it again. I won't give up. I thought, I don't know what you want, but you're not going to get me to respond to this. I'm not going to do it half-heartedly. Every time I do it, no matter how many times you make me do it, I'll do it the same. I'll do it as well each time. And fuck you. This is what's going on in here [*points to his head*]. 'Again!' The room was full of fifty people, half of whom were actors and the rest of them extras and crew. You could see the crew shuffling on their feet, feeling embarrassed. I didn't know what to do. It was a terrible situation I found myself in.

MG: What did he want?

GAMBON: I don't know. Never spoke to him about it. Never referred to it since.

MG: Sounds as if you were a prisoner of war and you were being tortured.

GAMBON: Yes. They're going to kill me. I remember this day. It was the worst day of my professional life. Then he just said, 'Print.' I walked away, and that was it. On about take twenty, something happened. I was told about it afterwards.

I was supposed to be speaking to the leaders of the Admiralty, making a plea. At the back of the hall the extras are sitting there dressed up as 18th-century gentlemen. I didn't know it, but over my shoulder in the frame, a few of the extras in the back – as they would after that number of takes – started giggling, breaking up. Apparently Bill Nighy, a friend of mine who was in it, on take twenty he went up to them, while they were changing the magazine, and he said, 'If you laugh again during the take, I'll break your fucking heads off.'

MG: And they didn't laugh again?

GAMBON: No.

MG: Why were they laughing?

GAMBON: Because they lose concentration, and the guy who does a speech for three minutes and breaks down crying – I think if I was them, I'd laugh.

MG: How could you do it so many times?

GAMBON: Interesting story, isn't it? It's an important scene. You can't fuck about with it. You can't say, I'm not going to do it well, or I'm going to make it funny. You've got to do it straight.

MG: As a challenge to the director?

GAMBON: If that's what he wanted, he didn't get it.

MG: As the star of this movie, you could have said that was the last take, you can use that one – or not.

GAMBON: That's what some people would have done. Knowing him as I know him, if I had done that, he would have gone berserk. He would have fallen apart. It was late, near the end of the shooting. If that's ever printed in a book, he'll probably deny it. I like him. He's an extremely clever man. I do mean that. So this episode is a mystery.

MG: So why did he do it?

GAMBON: I've thought about it for years, ever since that happened four, five years ago. I thought maybe he thinks I find acting too easy. That's what kept occurring to me. Because he thinks I find acting easy, he's going to make me find it difficult.

I heard a similar thing about a famous Hollywood actor in a film about pool playing, *The Hustler*. Is it Jackie Gleason who says 'You owe me money,' or is it Lee J. Cobb? [It was George C. Scott.] He screams it across the pool hall at Paul Newman, I think, when he realises Newman's been hustling. All these stories are apocryphal. Someone once told me the director made him do it forty times because he didn't want him to shout the line, 'You owe me money.' But the actor wouldn't do it as the director wanted. He thought eventually this man will run out of energy and he won't be able to shout it. So he'll do it the way I want him to do it. But he wouldn't. Every take the same. In the end, he has to print it. He's got nothing else.

MG: During rehearsals of *Death of a Salesman*, Lee J. Cobb was terrible, subdued, without life, and Kazan thought about firing him. Then, suddenly one day, he exploded on one line – and never stopped and soared through the play. It was one of the greatest moments in Arthur Miller's life.

GAMBON: He was just finding his way. Slowly but surely. Those people don't understand that. I understand that completely. I'm a slow worker. Very, very slow. And then all the pieces don't show up for three weeks, and then one day, they start clicking up. You begin to find some sticks to walk on, and some ideas, and suddenly, it's just like an engine starting up. Pmmmph! Off you go. It's like a big discovery. That's exactly the way to do it. And then when people are watching you, a paying audience, that's when he will put number two firing system into operation. Step up on that. Then you really go.

MG: Cobb left *Salesman* early and went to Hollywood.

GAMBON: Every night he did it, he probably didn't want to do it because he was frightened he wouldn't be as good as he was.

That's a common feeling. You go on Monday night, you're a big hit, get raves, big newspaper articles about you. You're an enormous success. You don't want to do it again. Every night then there's a terrible agony of hitting the button again.

MG: Did you feel that way in *A View from the Bridge*?

GAMBON: Yes. It was you! You wrote a thing about me which Michael Codron put outside the theatre. In letters that big. [On August 23, 1987, in an essay in the *New York Times*, headlined 'A Virtuoso Who Specializes in Everything,' I wrote 'Role for role, pound for pound, Michael Gambon is, arguably, the finest actor in the English theatre.'] I went to Codron and said, 'Please take that down because I can't go on the stage every night with that outside. I can't fucking live up to it. I cannot cope with it.' He said, 'No.' I said, 'Please.' Every night I went through agony. Every night I was Eddie Carbone an hour before the people arrived, full costume in the dressing room. And every night I didn't want to do it because I didn't want to spoil what people had said about me. It's true, it's the fact. You wrote something and it was outside. Codron never took it down. You were up there. It was letters that high and it was right alongside the Aldwych Theatre. Something deeply flattering. A fellow actor of mine would see it and say, 'Oh, fuck him.' It would annoy other actors. If someone had said that about Russell Beale, I'd hate that. No, I wouldn't. So maybe that's why Lee J. Cobb did that. I can understand that completely. He had a big hit. After a month of doing it, he thought, I don't want to do this anymore because I've done it. And I want to be a movie star.

MG: Sometimes a critic will describe a scene that he liked so vividly – I remember Walter Kerr did that about Donald Pleasence onstage in the dark in *The Caretaker.*

GAMBON: And spoiled it for Donald.

MG: And for the audience, which kept watching and wondering when this would happen, when this 'number' would come.

GAMBON: Which wasn't a number in the first place. Usually friends do it. When they come see you in a play and they say, 'I love that moment,' and you say, 'No, don't tell me.' As soon as people draw your attention to it . . .

MG: Often actors will say they don't read reviews. True?

GAMBON: They always say that, but it's not true. I don't read them to begin with. I'll wait for a few weeks, then get my agent to put them all in a pile. I say if there is anything that is not complimentary, don't put it in the pile. In other words, I never read bad ones. Reading bad reviews is not good for you. I think it's a good idea to have someone to vet them for you, and not read the bad ones.

MG: What do the bad ones do for you?

GAMBON: They just lower you, and you've got to go on tonight and do it again. It's not very healthy. You could just make a mental note of critics who constantly give you bad reviews and maybe arrange to have them murdered. Pay for his annihilation. Someone once told me that Steven Berkoff threatened one critic with a knife. I don't know how true that is. I'd like it to be true.

MG: You know the story about David Storey punching Michael Billington after he gave him a negative review, and saying that if he was going to tangle with him he should be in better shape.

GAMBON: Wow! Great! I approve of that. I think violence is good in that department. I went to the BAFTA awards for *The Singing Detective* and I sat with Dennis Potter. He threw a knife and a fork at the table where the judges were sitting and shouted out a few obscenities.

I got a bad review once from a critic, and years later he had written a series to be done on the radio. I was in a restaurant and he came towards me across the room and I made out I didn't know who he was. I wouldn't give him the pleasure of knowing who he was. He came up to me and said, 'Excuse me, Mr Gambon.' I said, 'Oh, hello.' He waited, and I said, 'Who are you?' He said, 'I'm so and so. I write for the . . . paper. I've just written a major new drama series for radio and I'd be thrilled if you would play the lead in it for me.' I said, 'That's very kind of you to do that, but I don't act anymore.' He stared at me. 'What do you mean?' I said, 'I had to give it up three months ago. I'm running an engineering company in Kingston upon Thames. A relative of mine has just died and I've had to take on the responsibility. So I've given up acting.' He said, 'So you can't do this series?' I said, 'No, I'm sorry. It's very kind of you, but it's not my bag anymore.' He said, 'Oh, thank you,' and walked away. It just came to me what to say to him. I had to hurt him, so I hurt him first by not knowing who he was and second by saying I couldn't be in his series because I didn't act anymore. That was good, wasn't it?

Usually I'm lucky with critics. They're kind to me. Except one little fucker, Nicholas de Jongh. He needs to be shot.

MG: Actors want to be loved?

GAMBON: I think there's a danger of wanting to be loved and playing parts in a way so that people like you. I've never done that. I'll go the other way. I want to play parts where the audience hates my guts. And I'll put a little extra stuff on there just to make sure. That's quite legitimate. I'm not saying you bend the text or the meaning of the author.

MG: You've played some rather unsympathetic characters, but offhand I can't think of having hated any of them.

GAMBON: Well, maybe that's my failing.

MG: No, no, the opposite. Even as you do that . . .

GAMBON: You introduce humanity. That's right. As it would be in life. Even the most terrible people must have some quality in them.

In that last interview with Melvyn Bragg, Dennis [Potter] mentioned me. He said, 'The Michael Gambon character.' That made me so happy. That's like going down in history.

MG: Now your play has closed, what do you do in the evening?

GAMBON: Last night I went to my Rowland Club dinner. We're all experts on firearms. We wear dinner jackets. We go to a very posh gentleman's club in the West End. We bring items from our collection. I brought in a beautiful pair of late-18th-century pocket pistols, London 1770, in a shagreen contour case, with silver clips. When it's your turn, you talk about them and pass them around the table. We're all quite advanced collectors, so some treasures turn up. My last meeting, I brought the most beautiful royal rifle that belonged to the Duke of York, who died in 1827. It was sold at Christie's in 1827, and it's come to me.

MG: Are you the only actor in the group?

GAMBON: The only actor. Thank god. Most of them are doctors and lawyers and businessmen and company directors.

MG: What did you think about that autopsy that was presented on television as a public event?

GAMBON: A public autopsy! Extraordinary. Mind you, I see nothing wrong with it. The man gave his permission: yes, do this when I'm dead. But I can't imagine what sort of people would pay money and sit and watch. Although on TV, in America and here, you do see operations, heart transplants, which I find fascinating. But here it's someone dead. It's verging on the arts. He's a bit of an artist. Doing the autopsy, he wore a trilby hat, a blue suit, rubber gloves, and fedora – with a scalpel. And all these Spitalfields-type people sitting around – trendy artists.

MG: And critics were there watching.

GAMBON: Of course. Back row, Nicholas de Jongh. [*Laugh.*]

MG: He wasn't on the slab.

GAMBON: I always want to say to critics, 'Why don't you mind your own fucking business?'

'When you're acting in a drama on stage, there's a little man in your head . . . talking to you all the time. He's saying, "That went well. Now bring it up a bit. Now bring it down" '

Gambon was having a busy year in the movies. He had finished his role in Sylvia (playing a neighbour to Gwyneth Paltrow as Sylvia Plath) and in Layer Cake, a British gangster film. He still had several days to go on Being Julia (with Annette Bening) and Harry Potter and the Prisoner of Azkaban, in which he replaced Richard Harris in the role of Dumbledore. Open Range, a Kevin Costner western in which Gambon played the villain, was about to be released. He seemed glad to have all the work, but regretted having nothing on tap in the theatre. We met at Orso and sat in the smoking section. He was curious about all the plays I was seeing in London and about others that he might do. I told him I was writing a piece about Nicholas Hytner and his first season as director of the National Theatre. He praised Hytner highly and said that Hytner had asked him to do Waiting for Godot, but that Peter Hall had the rights up to the fiftieth anniversary year of the first London production.

GAMBON: This year I've been doing *Harry Potter*, taking over from Richard. I enjoy that. It's about the children, you know, and if you're an adult in it, you hardly get used. I've been on it since early this year and I spend most of my time fretting because I'm not wanted. I think I've got four days more to do on that. It's fine when you're doing it, but I don't do it often enough. I think in the contract it says that the older actors do twenty-two days each or something like that, so I've been doing other things. I've done a film called *Layer Cake*, about London gangsters, made by the same producer who did *Lock, Stock and Two Smoking Barrels*. I've done a film with Istvan Szabo in Hungary called *Being Julia*, with Annette Bening, adapted from the Somerset Maugham novel, *Theatre*. Annette plays the actress and I play a ghost, her old director. And I'm supposed to be doing a film with Wes Anderson in Italy. *Harry Potter* is the main one and then I've been playing little parts in movies that people offer me. Most movies you make in England now are called low-budget films. They just say that so as not to give you any money.

MG: Low-budget means low-budget for the actors?

GAMBON: That's right. I find it all frustrating, leading nowhere, treading water. I don't know what to do. I feel at sea. I was talking to Ralph Fiennes the other night, and he said, his greatest joy is being in a theatre and being part of a company. I think it's mine as well, being with a group of people. I miss that. That's what I admire about Ralph. He's a movie star but he keeps on doing these big plays. He told me he wants to do Hamlet next – again. I think his movies finance his theatre career. I like his bravery [in Ibsen's *Brand*]. I like the way he stands on the stage with his feet foursquare and plays the part. It's a lovely simple production by Adrian Noble – there's no bullshit about it. The power of *Brand*! Ralph got a bit of humour in there as well, which I thought was clever.

MG: Tell me about your character in *Harry Potter*.

GAMBON: He's the headmaster and runs the shooting match. He's all-knowing although he pretends he doesn't know anything. He's quite subtly funny. The children love him; he's wonderful with kids. The first day of shooting I just went on to the set as Dumbledore, with the long beard and all the stuff that Richard wore. I started saying the lines and I couldn't stop not being Irish. I did the first scene and Alfonso Cuaron [the director] said to me, 'Is this Irish?' and I said yeah. He said, OK. So I've done it Irish. When I put the beard on, he seemed Irish. Quite a lyrical, poetic, nice man. We're a bit scruffier than the earlier films. I like Alfonso. He keeps the camera moving all the time. Great swooping crane shots. A load of money put into this. It'll look great. It's straight-forward, no subtext, but that's not what it's about. It's quite lyrical, some of it.

MG: In a movie with many villains, you're playing a good guy.

GAMBON: I should be one of the villains. The other actors are terrific: Tim Spall, Gary Oldman, David Thewlis, a really strong group of actors. I think it'll be brilliant. Fiona Shaw. Alan Rickman is there. I read the book of the one I'm doing, *The Prisoner of Azkaban.* I have to do two other Harry Potter movies after this. It's like having a bit of a pension. So I could do a bit more theatre. I was thinking: I'd like to find a really good new play and go to Michael Codron or Robert Fox and say, will you put this on? I suppose the RSC and the National and other companies get ten new plays a day. For once, I would just like to control my own life.

MG: You've always said before that you didn't want to look for a play, but just let things come to you.

GAMBON: I thought it would be a good thing to do, and if you could influence Michael Codron or Robert Fox or whoever it would be – why not? I've never done that before. I don't think Judi and Maggie do that. They blow with the wind like most people. You want something from the heart that's lying unused on some desk. Some great work of art.

MG: Many of your characters have not been flamboyant – as in *A Number* and in the Ayckbourn plays.

GAMBON: They're back-foot characters. I like that sort of character. That isn't flamboyant, that's subdued.

MG: Do you have any more television coming up?

GAMBON: I did those three series on the trot and I haven't had an inkling since.

MG: Tell me about working with Annette Bening.

GAMBON: She's great. I had the scene with her where she has to come into the room crying, really crying. I have a speech to her in a mirror in her dressing table while she's crying. I found that really hard. Annette prepares herself and on 'action' she comes on the set and she cries for real, and if I blow it we've got to do it again. I had to hang on tight because I'm not used to that sort of reality. I suppose because I'm a theatre actor. I play a dead man who keeps reappearing to her, who was her original mentor and discovered her. Kind of Svengali. I'm still working on it.

MG: When I saw Deborah Warner in New York, she praised you very highly.

GAMBON: I love her. She's the most attractive woman I know. She's mindbogglingly attractive. In fact when I'm with her, I can hardly breathe. Just her being, the way she sits, the way she talks, I find rather overwhelming.

MG: She said about you: 'One of the greatest actors there ever ever was. He is absolutely the essence of the thing, but he gets bored very quickly.' And she explained how in the movie she made with you, she gave you this generator to play with. She said it was up to the director to keep you interested. She said she would love to do a play with you.

GAMBON: I'd love to do a play with her. But I do get bored. I think it's unnatural to do a play eight times a week. There are only a few a week when you really feel as though you're up and you've got the command of it. But maybe it's built up in your own mind. You think you're worse than you are. There's always a level, but you can hear what it should be, you can feel what it should be, so you think you're miles out, but you needn't be miles out.

MG: In our conversations, sometimes you've told me three or four different versions of various stories. When *The Singing Detective* won the BAFTA awards, who threw what at whom?

GAMBON: I think what happened was that Dennis Potter was at our table and at the other were the judges, and when he didn't get the award, which was an absolute fucking disgrace, Dennis threw a fork under the other table. And then when he went to go to the bathroom, I went with him. And up on the first floor corridor at the Dorchester Hotel, there was Joan Collins with two bodyguards. He said to her, 'Joan, I'd like to fuck you.' [*Laughs.*] And the two bodyguards went for him. She said, 'No, leave him alone. The man's a genius. He can fuck me whenever he wants to.'

MG: Your story about auditioning for Olivier changes in the telling.

GAMBON: Yes, as time goes on and you get older, it alters slightly. The elements are true.

MG: Having a 'heart attack' while flying with Terence Rigby, throwing the samovar – those stories were true. And your Oscar Wilde stories about rushing on the train in costume.

GAMBON: I don't believe half those stories. I don't feel I could do any of them, but it must be in moments of great emotion I do these things. It was me, but it's not the me sitting here. The idea of running through Bristol dressed as Oscar Wilde with a gold cane and a wig covered in make-up, in costume from 1890, is unbelievable. I can't conceive of doing it. The anger in me must have been so powerful.

MG: And the story about *Ghosts* and the moving table?

GAMBON: They're the two worst corpsers in the world – Judi Dench and Ken Branagh. Can't keep a straight face in anything they've ever done.

MG: We're seeing Branagh tonight in David Mamet's *Edmond.*

GAMBON: I saw that. He's terrific. He's another actor I like very much. The play is just a series of events of a man going up the wall. No big deal. It's very well written and it's funny and the production is great.

MG: What happened to your film, *The Actors*?

GAMBON: That was a massive flop. I went to the premiere in Dublin. It was a big do. We all stayed in the U2 hotel by the Liffey, and then we went to the premiere in limos. I came back to London and waited for it to open properly. [*He groans.*]

MG: It wasn't good?

GAMBON: I couldn't stop laughing. I thought it was a charming, beautiful, funny Irish film, but they didn't like it. Disappeared. Maybe it'll come out on video. Maybe it'll become a cult film. I don't say one line without the word fuck in it. I find myself very funny in it. I was laughing at me. I did everything in the part that I knew I'd find funny. And if I find it funny then presumably most people would find it funny. The way he moves, the way he dressed, the sort of things he says. Conor [McPherson, who was the director and screenwriter] is quite free about dialogue. You can make up your own bit now and again if you want to. He keeps the camera running.

MG: Is your character an actor?

GAMBON: No, he's a nightclub owner and part-time criminal, with no brain whatsoever. With two grown-up sons, both mentally backward. Between the three of us, we created very funny things. This is a supporting part. Michael Caine plays the lead. Anyway, it's a flop.

MG: Do you often laugh at yourself like that?

GAMBON: Yeah. Like in a theatre when you're onstage playing a comedy, you're doing things that would make you laugh
– without bending the character too much. When I did Ayckbourn, I'd do things that I know if I were sitting there
watching, I'd laugh at. That's the way you do it. You do things
that would make you laugh. In drama, you're acting the way
you would really like to sound and look, but all the time you
can hear yourself missing it. When you're acting in drama on
stage, there's a little man in your head looking at you, talking
to you all the time, he's coming to you in your brain about
how a scene's just gone, and how you look, and how you can
tell a story just by the movement of a head. It's not the same
in a comedy; it's another world.

MG: A little man in your head?

GAMBON: Yes, he's talking all the time. He's saying, 'That
went well, that was good. Now, bring it up a bit. Now bring it
down. No, that's boring. Now, do this. It will look good if you
went like that. Now stay like that. Now turn like that.' All actors
have that. I think. Because that's how you act – somebody
inside is directing you. Your judge is there, your sense of taste,
and your sense of rhythm, your sense of how you sound and
whether you're being cheap or not telling the truth. When
you're talking to somebody on the stage and suddenly you
undercut them. He might say, 'No that's cruel, don't do that
again.'

MG: When you do comedy, there's no little man.

GAMBON: No, the little man is not there.

MG: He's busy?

GAMBON: He's somewhere else. He's like the dramaturge.
He's gone out, he's having a smoke in the corridor. I'm sure
that all actors who play comedy do things that they would
laugh at.

MG: Do you surprise yourself when you play comedy?

GAMBON: No, I don't. But sometimes the laugh surprises you. Some things get a big laugh and you don't know why and so you hang on to it closely.

MG: And in playing the dramatic roles?

GAMBON: Well over a five or six-week rehearsal, things occur to you. Like building blocks. When we did *Galileo*, I wore clothes to rehearsal every day, baggy pants and a shirt, and then I put a cloak on. Then I always resent not having to wear those clothes anymore. You become so attached to them. When you do the big leap from the rehearsal room onto the stage, you put costumes on. I find that's the most traumatic time of all. You want to keep those other clothes. I remember when I did Lear, I wanted to wear what I had been wearing in the rehearsals. I mentioned that to Adrian Noble once. You get so fond of the stuff. Actors turn up in clothes they think would be appropriate, even in Shakespeare. What if they just left them on in the production?

In *A Number*, Daniel and I would turn up for rehearsal with sort of what we would wear in the show. My character wore a suit and Daniel wore a T-shirt and jeans. So I wore a suit to rehearsal and he wore jeans and we almost just walked from the rehearsal room at the Court down onto the stage and did it. That was one of the attractions about that show: the transfer was so easy. Before the first night Stephen took us round to a girls school in Chelsea, literally around the corner, about fifty girls – 15, 16 years old – and we said we want to do a play for you. This was in the afternoon. We arranged all the chairs. We were just wearing our own clothes – no lights and no cues. And we just did it. And it was great. We were really close to the kids, which I ordinarily don't like because I like the artifice of the theatre, the curtain and the lights. But this was really extraordinary. In that play you have no props. You have two chairs, one at the back, one at the front, and nothing else. I think when I got to the cigarette, I didn't light it because of the kids. I just lay there. It's lovely having that freedom. You could do *A Number* anywhere. You could do it now, over there, for these people there, and you could do it in movie conversational tones. You wouldn't have that element of theatricality about it. In the theatre, you would do that. But in an environment like here, it's like a movie.

MG: Do you ever watch your movies?

GAMBON: No. I watched *The Singing Detective* a few times. I liked that.

MG: You know they remade that with Robert Downey Jr.

GAMBON: How could you make a film of that in two hours? It's seven hours. Why do it? The story is complicated, and that's its joy.

MG: They remake a lot of things.

GAMBON: Why? Has there ever been a remake that's better than the original? Although some remakes make money, the one with De Niro, *Cape Fear.*

MG: We're seeing *His Girl Friday* at the National. That's a remake of a remake.

GAMBON: I saw that. It's funny, it's witty. The man who plays the lead, a proper stage actor, Alex Jennings. He's great. He's everything a stage actor should be. He's got presence, you could hear him. He's funny, he moves well, he's a great object lesson for kids to go and see and watch how to do it. He's terrific – style, verve – and Zoë Wanamaker, very good.

MG: What are you doing the rest of the week?

GAMBON: Tomorrow I've got a voice-over for a bank. Monday I go back to *Being Julia*, filming in London. On Friday I go to Jersey where I do a scene with Annette, my last scene in the film. Then I have a photo shoot for *Harry Potter* the next day. Then I go back into *Harry Potter* for four days shooting. The older I get, I get more work in films, playing old fuckers.

The drug film I just did, they said, 'You've got to go to Saville Row to be fitted for a suit.' I said no. They said, 'We'll give you

195

the suit.' I said all right. I went – three different fittings over three weeks for the suit, cost £3000. It's so perfect, you don't even know you've got it on. HBO gave me eight Lyndon Johnson suits – and those suits cost 2000 bucks each.

MG: Do you ever wear them?

GAMBON: No, I wouldn't wear them. They're so old-fashioned. I just had to have them – because they were free. I've got forty-eight suits. Did I tell you what I did in Lyndon Johnson? The set photographer was on the stage one day. He said, 'Mike, put your feet up on the Oval Office desk.' He then took the photograph. There he's got the President of the United States with the seal of office behind me, and right there my shoes up on the desk. It says 'Allen Edmonds high-class shoes'. Allen Edmonds is a famous American shoe-maker. So we sent it to the CEO of Allen Edmonds, and he went ape shit. 'Send this man shoes.' I got three pairs of Allen Edmonds shoes and the driver of my car in LA said, 'Get me a pair of golf shoes. I'm size 8.' Then one of the cameramen said, 'Get me some sneakers.' I had everyone on the set coming to me. I said I can't send for the shoes for different sizes. A big box arrived with the shoes.

MG: At home you have all these suits and shoes.

GAMBON: They're in racks. It's like a tribute to a man who doesn't know what to do with himself. It's just the idea of getting something for nothing.

MG: You live in Gravesend?

GAMBON: That's where Pocahontas is buried. The best examples of varying English architecture anywhere in the country, from late-17th-century to modern day.

MG: Tell me about your house.

GAMBON: It's big. It's Queen Anne. It's 1716. Then at one end there are 19th-century additions, built around 1820. Eight acres.

MG: Your house once belonged to Lord Nelson?

GAMBON: So they say. Up on one of the walls it says, '1805, the Battle of Trafalgar'. It's quite near where he used to moor his ships. Part of the house looks like a ship. There is a connection there somewhere, I like to think. I don't know for sure. Local word of mouth says he used to stay there.

MG: Have you finished your pre-computer toolroom?

GAMBON: It's almost done. I need two more pieces of equipment to make it a pre-CNC toolroom, Computer Network Control, which is what the world goes on. And then I've achieved my ambition.

MG: Why do you need such a large house?

GAMBON: I don't know. When the property slump came, it was cheap. I bought it. Now it's gone up again. I'm going to sell it and move back again into central London. Kensington. I like the streets and the pavement and the noise.

MG: You'd need a big garage for your cars.

GAMBON: I know. They'd have to go. I came in in a Ferrari today. I couldn't have that in London. It's not a London car. I'd like to begin to simplify life. Pare down. Little house. Get an ordinary little car, park it in the street. Do you remember Diana Dors? She once said to me, if you ever do well in this business, you'll be tempted to buy a big house. Don't! She's right. It's a waste of time. It's a beautiful house, though, classic English Georgian house, like every picture postcard of England.

'I became an actor because I wanted to be behind the curtain. I wanted to be in the secret world of the curtain and the stage door and the backstage and the other world – and with the audience out there. I like to retain the mystery'

Back at Orso, I began by telling him I had run into Deborah Warner at a performance of Edmond *at the National Theatre.*

MG: I told her that I had seen you and you had said that you loved her. She said, 'He's tried that before.'

GAMBON: She didn't!

MG: What does that mean?

GAMBON: Wow, oh wow. She wasn't upset by that?

MG: No.

GAMBON: You know what she used to call me at the National? Her fiancé. Even before I knew her very well, she used to say, 'Oh, there's my fiancé over there.' I would hear her saying it when I was queuing up for my lunch. Did you like *Edmond*? The play's about something we all know about – New York and a big city and what happens to a man, but as a piece of theatre it's good.

MG: I agree and Branagh gave a very brave performance.

GAMBON: Absolutely. Body language, and I liked the way he characterised it. He had some wonderful physicalities there – his stance. A surprising actor. The play is written in broad strokes and I think Ken's performance was in broad strokes.

MG: In Antony Sher's autobiography [*Beside Myself*], he writes about rehearsing *Lear* with you. He said that you practised the storm scenes on Dover's Hill outsider Chipping Campden, with you 'roaring at jets passing from the nearby airbase.'

GAMBON: Adrian Noble told us to do that. He would take us out in a car. We would do scenes in the middle of an open gravel pit. Just shouting at each other. I don't know whether it's useful. It gives you an idea of what it's like to speak in the open air, rather than in the confines and formality of the stage. Then you don't need to do that anymore because you learn how to do it.

MG: Sher also talks about the music-hall routines, your 'ability to switch from clowning with his Fool to the terrible rages with his daughters, and then the disintegration into confusion and vulnerability.'

GAMBON: That's the joy of those parts. That's why they're so great because no actor could ever fill them properly. I've seen *King Lear*, and some actors aren't good at the beginning because they can't do the rage. You're looking for a way into it and you can't find one. The initial rage when he banishes and attacks Cordelia – the way the logic of my mind works, I couldn't find how to do that to make it real. So when you do it, the little man in your head is saying, I don't believe you, and he keeps saying that. So the first part of the play for me was terribly difficult.

MG: How did you finally do it?

GAMBON: You just have to do it, and you find out at the end of the evening that maybe you got away with it. The second half of the play is what I love, the reborn Lear, the Lear that goes on the heath and wakes up. The whole end of the play is more attractive to me than the first half. When I've seen *King Lear*, I always find that true.

MG: The problem is to believe that Lear will banish his favourite daughter.

GAMBON: Yes, that's what I have a problem with. It's a dramatic device that every actor who has played it has had to cope with it. You find different ways around the problem. Sometimes the director solves it. He does something on the stage that helps the actor. It's very difficult. I remember someone gave me a stone, a polished pebble and I used that.

MG: You mentioned that before and I didn't understand: you would hold it?

GAMBON: In my pocket, in my hand.

MG: How would that help you?

GAMBON: It would give me something to hold on to. I felt secure with it. But I lost it.

MG: You lost it? Like Richardson and his box, when he lost his 'talent'?

GAMBON: I lost the stone! [*Loud laugh.*]

MG: Somewhere on the way to the RSC?

GAMBON: I lost it. I never found it again. But I found another stone in a garden somewhere, and I used that.

MG: I was just over at the Theatre Museum and your stone is on exhibition there, with a sign, 'Gambon's Stone.'

GAMBON [*continues laughing*]: Yes.

MG: Would Noble have helped you with that part of the play?

GAMBON: I can't remember the process, but he did. I think I upset Tony when we came to London. I wanted to change things and it seemed like I was in a well-oiled machine. Instead of confronting the change I wanted to do, I didn't tell anyone, I just did it.

MG: I saw it at Stratford but not in London. How was it different?

GAMBON: I didn't fool around so much with the clown. The front-cloth scenes I played more down. I played the last half of the run in Stratford without Tony. Tony broke his Achilles tendon. I think I got into a rhythm with the other guy then, that wasn't so challenging for me, and when we got to London [with Sher returning to his role], I kept doing it as I had been doing it there. I changed bits, but it was never as fulfilling.

MG: Sher hints that maybe you changed things in response to the fact that he got such great reviews as the Fool.

GAMBON: I can't remember my emotions at the time, but I think that might be true, that I wanted to reassert myself.

MG: I would have thought that the most difficult part of Lear for an actor would be when he's mad, on the heath.

GAMBON: I found that easier somehow. The madness appealed to me. I could understand that. This man goes through this turmoil. It's like he's got dementia. He gets out on the heath and he goes over the top. I didn't find that as difficult as Lear with the daughters.

MG: What do you know about dementia?

GAMBON: I can just imagine. My dog has it. I know he does. The vet told me. He's 12 or 13 now, and he's losing brain

201

cells. He doesn't know where he is. He doesn't know who you are. When I've met old people with dementia, you can see the fear in their eyes. They know there's something deeply wrong with them. And their panic is overwhelming, then suddenly [*snaps his fingers*] they're all right for a few minutes. Which makes it all the worse. Eventually what happens with dementia, I'm told – the flash ceases to happen. And you go into a tunnel of nothingness. I suppose that's when old people are happier.

MG: They don't remember their angers and animosities.

GAMBON: I believe they become quite calm.

MG: Sher said that great acting is 'about contradictions and conflict . . . opposites in our nature, living side by side, yet often at war: the adult and the child, the animal and the intellect, the male and the female.' Contradictions and conflict?

GAMBON: All that. I don't really know how it works. I know that if you're in a great play and you're cast properly, then you're lucky. Sometimes you find yourself doing things and you don't know why you're doing them. But they're right. If you centralise the role, you can take off with it because you've got that freedom in a great play. There were some bits in *Skylight*, which I thought were very well written and beautiful. As the run went on, we did all sorts of things with those sections of the play that the director and author, I think, quite liked, and never commented on. David's characters have a lot of depth. That gives you freedom. I suppose that's when you can be a great actor, when you can ride a play properly and put everything into it, without confusing the audience. Ken [Branagh in *Edmond*] is really having fun with it. He's intelligent enough to know where he can root around. And maybe Ed Hall [the director] contributes to that.

MG: You found it in *Lear*, *Antony*, *Galileo*, *Skylight*.

GAMBON: If I'm lucky, I'll find it somewhere.

MG: I understand what you say about Eddie Carbone and about the character in *Skylight*, but it's a great leap to go to Lear and Galileo.

GAMBON: Oh, they're the same, I think. The same fundamental crisis of people.

MG: Their emotions seem larger.

GAMBON: Yes. They're big. It's just a different level of emotions. What I like about Eddie Carbone is that we would play the play for its American realism, its street realism. But it can also take a bit of what we English guys do – classical acting. You can really roll on that.

MG: I recently saw the opera version of *A View of the Bridge*. The play is kind of operatic.

GAMBON: Yes. So maybe I like plays that are operatic. I remember in *A View from the Bridge*, I did a ballet leap in it. I don't know how I got it in. A drama student up north wrote to me, 'I saw you do it, but I couldn't believe it. You did a balletic leap from one side of the stage to the other during a scene change.' I think the happier you feel in a part, the more you can do.

MG: You talk about combining the American with the classical, in contrast to some other English actors.

GAMBON: I like to slide a bit of the other stuff in. It makes it more fun and more interesting for the audience. I think it's part of the game to add as much as you can to it. That's what I love about the Scottish play, when he comes out of the room having murdered the king, that bit of Pinteresque dialogue there. That's pure Pinter: when, where, how. And if you do that like it's real and it's conversational, I suppose that's what you're trying to achieve.

MG: That makes you sound more like an American actor.

GAMBON: I'm obsessed by American actors. That's who I would like to be. If I was born differently, a different shape

203

and a different look, I'd like to be . . . an American film star [as well as a ballet dancer]. I would! I think that's the best of all. If you look like the sort of guy who could be an American movie star, and you could also act in the English traditional way – my god, think of the things you could do.

MG: Was there anybody who did that?

GAMBON: No, I can't think of anyone. But if you kept it a dark secret, you could slide it into movies, you'd be the best actor in the world. Laurence Olivier wasn't a brilliant movie actor, was he? But, my god, he was a stage actor beyond belief.

MG: Al Pacino tries to do both.

GAMBON: I saw Al in *Hughie*. I liked that very much. I liked the way he encompassed the stage. It surprised me a bit. When I first saw him in London in *American Buffalo* – he's a good stage actor. He knows the rules. He's rather obsessed by theatre.

MG: Is there anything you could say to young actors?

GAMBON: I'd be better with younger actors if I knew a scene from a play, and they were doing that scene, and I watched it and showed them what I'd do, or how I'd approach it, or what I did at a particular moment, or how they could feel freer with it, how they could relax. Helping young actors? I could only do it by demonstration. Or I could direct things by adjusting shapes.

MG: You've said that physicality was very important.

GAMBON: And that's something one does intuitively in rehearsals. I enjoy that. I particularly liked that in *A Number*, staying close and breaking away, and suddenly you find yourself in like a dance. At the same time, the two guys are speaking quite normally to each other.

MG: Do you make notes on your scripts?

GAMBON: Yes. They're all very simple notes, usually about where I'm moving to, and I usually put marks where I've got a change of thoughts. I put a big cross where something really important happens. I have my own little dingles. At the National with Olivier, we used to write in our scripts the way he did. He'd go DLC. Down Left Centre. UL. Up Left. DR. Down Right. The stage is split into the centre line. Up Centre is here. Down Right Centre is here. [*Indicates on the table.*] That's so old-fashioned, it's almost Victorian. I still do that. I still write ULC, DR. I always know the lines by where I am on the stage.

At Stratford we had two weeks off, because other plays were opening. *Lear* closed on a Saturday and didn't play again for two weeks, and I didn't look at the script once. We came back on the following Monday. I stood in the wings and that terrible fear, overwhelming fear came over me because I had deliberately not looked at it. I had that terrible fear, but I walked on and, boof, out it comes.

I don't know what I would say to young actors: they should stay on the stage for a good few years before they try to do anything else. It's a good background for everything else, for film acting, for television acting. It teaches you how to act with your whole body. Having said that, all those wonderful American film stars didn't do that, yet they're OK.

MG: Somebody is going to read this and say, what about his personal, away-from-theatre life? What about it?

GAMBON [*smiles and then draws an imaginary zipper across his mouth, and laughs*]: I always say people should look after their own affairs.

MG: Are you still married?

GAMBON [*softly*]: Yeah. I never speak . . .

MG: But people do wonder.

GAMBON: Why don't they mind their own business? It's fuck-all to do with them. This is a book about acting in the theatre, about being an actor. This thing about being well known, or being a celebrity, is one of the awkward things about being an actor. I like to be an actor in the same way that Joe Bloggs is a bus driver.

MG: But people want to know more about the actors they admire.

GAMBON: Yeah. Why? It's so sad. I always think, get a life. Who gives a fuck?

MG: The audience does.

GAMBON: Well, get a life. I feel sorry for them.

MG: They come to feel possessive of a person.

GAMBON: I think it gets worse, the more we go on. Certainly in this country, the cult of celebrity and fame has become obscene. Kids don't want to do real jobs anymore, they want to be actors or they want to be singers or dancers, or they want to be involved in what they call 'the media'.

MG: They also feel the money is there.

GAMBON: Ah, well. That's not a good reason for wanting to be an actor – money – because the likelihood is you'll never get it.

MG: I understand the fact that you don't want to talk about your private life. But people do want to know.

GAMBON: I get a lot of amusement out of it as well. Refusing to talk about it makes me laugh.

MG: You changed agents.

GAMBON: Only once in my life. I was with Larry Dalzell for twenty-five years, and then one day I left him. I went to ICM to Harriet Robinson, and I've been with Harriet now for seven or eight years. They say changing agents is like changing deck chairs on the Titanic.

MG: Why did you change agents?

GAMBON: It happened after I just went to LA. I found myself queuing up at the American embassy at seven o'clock in the morning to get a visa and I thought if I had a different sort of agent I wouldn't have to do this. My agent, although he was a wonderful fellow, didn't want to cope with all that sort of stuff. That's why American actors have managers.

MG: Are you bothered by people recognising you?

GAMBON: I get mainly recognised by older women, the main backbone of the National Theatre. Trevor Nunn said once when he was managing it, 'This is a great place to mingle with the elderly.'

MG: Deborah Warner said that Fiona Shaw is very conscious of who is in the audience. You don't ask who's out there.

GAMBON: No, I ask the company manager not to tell me. Some actors like to know.

When Deborah Warner was doing *Richard II* at the National, she called Paul Scofield and said, 'I'd like you to play John of Gaunt,' and he said, 'Who's playing Richard II?' She said, 'Fiona Shaw.' He said, 'Ohh. Why don't you ask Miriam Margolyes?'

MG: In Sher's book, he talks about the fact that after a performance of *Lear* in Stratford, you would all gather in the Dirty Duck.

GAMBON: And go completely berserk.

MG: He quotes Pete Postlethwaite saying about you, 'It's not fair, it's like acting next to a fucking cinema screen!'

GAMBON: He said that? We used to have such fun. Sometimes you get a bit annoyed by intellectuals who congregate at Stratford, teaching and children's groups and American university professors. One night we were in the Duck and there were four old guys, American professors of English literature, grey-haired, and they came over to me and they said, 'We've just seen the *King Lear*. How did you approach it?' Sher and Pete Postlethwaite were standing around and I suddenly went, no brain [*he speaks in a monotone*]: 'Well,

I went into London. I read the script and I realised he's not very happy. And so . . . ' And their faces were like [*he looks awestruck*]. Sher and Pete had to go, and I was trapped, I couldn't get out of it. The guys couldn't make it out. And I kept on with this brainless actor playing King Lear who hadn't got a thought in his head. They said, 'What about the resurrection of Cordelia?' I said, 'He's asleep.' It got worse and worse. I don't think they knew I was fooling them. And then you feel guilty. Nice people who were just interested. You can't help it.

MG: That reminds of the time that Pinter and I were doing a public conversation at the Lincoln Center and someone in the audience asked him, 'What is the purpose of your work?' – and Harold ended the discussion.

GAMBON: What sort of question is that? Harold's work stands there on its legs for you to watch. It's not up to him to tell you. And I think the same with acting. The actor goes on the stage to play the part. Now everyone wants to know all about it. They want you to go on the stage afterwards and meet children after *King Lear*, and tell them what it's all about. They've just seen the play.

MG: Sometimes with the schoolchildren, there's an honest attempt to indoctrinate a new audience.

GAMBON: I became an actor because the curtain's there in the auditorium, and I wanted to be behind the curtain. I wanted to be in the secret world of the curtain and the stage door and the backstage and the other world – and with the audience out there. And now there seems to be too much of this going on. I like to retain the mystery.

I've got to do a play next year – or go mad. It's the longest time I've been away. Theatre is my job. Films are just jam on the bread. I pine for the theatre sometimes. It's like going home – being on the stage.

Afterword

During previews of Cressida (*in 2000*), *a letter addressed to Gambon was left at the stage door of the Albery Theatre. It was an official-looking document printed on British Actors Equity stationery, and it posed a threat to the actor. Under a heading, 'Society of Word Perfect,' an organisation based in Geneva, there was a list of various dignitaries who supported this cause. As Nicholas Hytner (who directed the play) and others remembered, the letter read:*

Dear Sir Michael,

I am the acting president of a new joint subcommittee of British Actors Equity and the British Writers Guild. Over recent years, our respective unions have decided that enough is enough, it's time for Actors Equity to act on behalf of our brothers and sisters in the Writers Guild in upholding standards of verbal fidelity among our members. Therefore we have formed a committee which will monitor textual inaccuracies in the West End. You, Sir Michael, have been chosen as our first guinea pig. Members of our joint committee will be attending a performance of *Cressida*. We have been provided with copies of the script. We will be following it to find out if you are indeed word perfect, and we will report back to our committee.

The letter went on to say that the report would be published in *The Stage* and if there were three digressions from the text, the actor would be fined; if there were four, he would be banned from the profession. The letter was signed Martin Aston.

Hytner said that when Gambon read it, he exploded in outrage. 'It's a scandal,' he said. 'It's a fucking disgrace.' And he probably thought back to all the times he had indeed departed from a script. Several nights later, somebody at the stage door called Gambon in his dressing room and said, 'Sir Michael, Mr Aston from Word Perfect has been in tonight, and he wants to see you.' Mr Aston came backstage and to Gambon's relief, he turned out to be the actor Douglas Hodge, who was soon to play the role of Aston opposite Gambon in *The Caretaker.* In other words, this was a case of the trickster tricked. One could imagine the offstage laughter of Terence Rigby, Simon Russell Beale and all the others who had been victims of Gambon pranks.

Such tomfoolery has not distracted Gambon from his central purpose: to act his roles to the hilt. In December 2003, he was in Rome still working on that Wes Anderson film. Reached on his mobile telephone, he said that his career was 'a moveable feast,' at that moment more moveable than feast. But there was an exciting role on his horizon, in *Endgame*, directed by Matthew Warchus. Having played Hamm for television in the Gate Theatre, Dublin, series of all Beckett's stage plays, he was looking forward with heightened anticipation to bringing the character alive onstage. In the television version, steeped in an Irish accent and with a commanding Lear-like presence, Gambon captured the tragic dimensions of this deposed monarch approaching finality. He also uncovered the mordant humour, as exemplified by the line (uttered by Hamm's mother), 'Nothing is funnier than unhappiness, I grant you that.' Significantly it was with *Endgame*, and his kinsman Samuel Beckett that Michael Gambon returned to the theatre after a hiatus in films.

Conversations about Gambon

Alan Ayckbourn, 22 June 1990

It's not an accurate parallel, but he does have that slight curse of the Alec Guinnesses, as a man who for many years disappeared behind his roles. Gambon's self is there, as indeed with all great actors. But he is an extremely self-effacing actor onstage, which, in a sense, is not the usual image of a star – and he is terribly versatile and flexible and he does submerge himself. When you see him a lot you begin to know him and see what he does, but he doesn't bring on that 'me-me-me.' He brings on the man. I don't think he'd like the idea of having to inhabit a character with his own personality. He loves the idea of adopting roles. I think he's a character actor in the terms that Olivier was a character actor.

He's an intensely private man, a man who almost jealously guards his own privacy, his own self. He's very shy. He takes the work very seriously but he doesn't take himself too seriously. He has a wicked humour, and he has a hatred of pretension in theatre. He always says he feels safe with me directing. Working with him is like having some wonderful, limitless machine, like a Lamborghini, at your disposal as director and writer. He's a complete actor.

I think we work in a conspiratorial way. We steal up on characters. We were all slightly awed by him playing Eddie [in *A View from the Bridge*]. Having worked with him very closely on that, and then suddenly, this sort of massive eruption happened as a result of all the fuses one had lit. This huge performance came out, which was really quite daunting to be near.

211

He loves actors. He loves acting. But I think it's a craft for him, in the same way I think of playwriting as a craft. He doesn't like the cheap or the flashy that fool people. He's never attempted to use tricks to try and make a comic point. He said, 'I can only play it one way, and I'm going to play it true.' Sometimes he'll joke it up a bit for rehearsal, but in essence he'll play straight down the middle, and that's exactly the best comic acting. Great comedy is great truth and most great comic actors are great serious actors. There's not a division; there shouldn't be. He has that extraordinary range. There's nobody else that has a comparable ability to play quite so lightly and yet suddenly put on the power.

Harold Pinter, 25 June 1990

When Liv Ullmann played in *Old Times* at the Haymarket, Gambon was the man. David Jones [who directed the production] and I just looked at him and said, 'It's Michael Gambon we want,' because we knew as an actor he could do anything.

In a very short space of time, he played this extremely complex, introverted self-loathing man in *The Heat of the Day* [on television], full of doubt and despair and thwarted love, and at absolutely the same time he was playing this sergeant in my play [*Mountain Language*], who was totally without feelings, just a killer.

One of the things that he and I both share, having worked together so many times, is a concern about the physical state of affairs, where you are actually are. If you are in the wrong place, or you can't find a way of getting to that place, you have to keep burrowing away. I feel as a director that I would like you the actor to get from there to there. The question is how you can justify it so that it's harmonious and true and coherent, where it isn't arbitrary.

And I think we work terribly easily together. We just look at the thing itself and get on with it. His way of working is continually alive.

There is no question about it: over the past fourteen years, a great actor has come about. He really has just about everything – enormous power, great depth, absolute expertise and the ability to illuminate comically the character and the event by the simplest of means. He doesn't elaborate, he's not a theorist, he doesn't complicate. He goes for the heart of the matter, and does it most economically and totally without sentimentality. He can arrest and compel. At the centre of all this, he is a most delicate actor. I've worked with Olivier, Richardson, Gielgud, Scofield, Redgrave, Guinness and Peggy Ashcroft, the greats of English acting, and Michael Gambon is in that category.

Adrian Noble, 25 June 1990

King Lear probably remains for me one of the two or three most exciting rehearsal periods I've ever had in my life, largely because of Michael's absolute willingness to experiment with the play and to give every character, every other actor the right to find his own way. And so we went on this extraordinary journey, and we did very, very difficult exercises.

He can sometimes do a line and you hear it for the first time. That, in a way, is a definition of a great actor. He's like the old lightning flashing.

I really believe that he created a man whose madness was always there. Great actors aren't just great because they can deliver an extraordinary performance; they're great because they make other people great around them. He has the credentials and the potential to be one of that very, very small charmed circle of greats. He's just outside it because he doesn't believe it. He thinks acting is just mucking about. He has phenomenal technique, I mean real, real craft. He's an amazing technician. It's skill and imagination linked to his voice and his body. There's something bionic about him.

What is his range? On the one hand, it's wounded kings, and I don't just mean King Lear. I'm talking about something more mythical. On the other hand, it's ordinary people who have an absolutely unique quality about them. He has a great majesty and he also has that extraordinary ordinariness, which has flecks of genius. That's a marvellous gift.

Dennis Potter, 29 June 1990

MG: Was Gambon what you imagined for the role in *The Singing Detective*?

POTTER: He became so. He displaced any other thoughts one might have had. I don't see actors, as it were, in my head when I'm writing. But from the very first reading – and it was a huge part – he occupied it. There is something so deceptive about him. He's a bit like an old pair of shoes in some ways. They're your favourite and you can walk a long way in them. There's something almost stodgy and puddingy at one's first perception of him. Then there's that incredible lightness and skill and grace. He's a very un-actory actor. He's also a very shy man, which is useful. Shy people look at the world more carefully, I think.

MG: What were the essentials for an actor playing the role?

POTTER: That almost impossible thing to describe. A lack of self-consciousness. *The Singing Detective* character had to be both the singer in front of the band and a sick patient trying to reassemble himself in the hospital. Thirdly, is in the non-singing part of the fictive Singing Detective – he also had to be a pseudo-American tough guy. There couldn't be any element of duplicity, even when he was playing hackneyed, stereotypical detective-like asides. He had to do them as though they were real, even though he knew and the script demanded that they were also parody. There is a very fine line between parody, which is always boring and painful, and living within a parody and knowing it's a parody. It's just playing that role until you can start to relax and be whatever it is you are. That's very difficult to get to as an actor. There's something amazing about the ease in which Gambon can get to those places. If you looked at him walking along the street, you would say that his feet are slightly too heavy, that he had a couple of pounds of lead weight in them. That would be your first glimpse of him in your mind. Yet there's this nimbleness. The contrast between the immediate physical perception of him and what he can do is very wide indeed. He's an astonishingly good actor.

MG: It must have been difficult for him to play so many scenes in bed, to be confined like that and not be able to use all his faculties.

POTTER: He used his eyes in amazing fashion. His face was a battlefield in that bed. If I were an actor, I'd have thought being confined would be something I would prefer. Then you've really got to show what your face and eyes can do.

MG: Were you there for much of the filming?

POTTER: I was rather out of action for a lot of it. It was only in the first grappling with it that I was really present at all. I do remember at the read-through feeling vaguely unsettled by the fact that Gambon's eyes were never ever off me [*laughs*], sitting on the other side of the table and quite some feet away from him. I thought he was analysing my physical – I don't think he was as crude as that – but I think he was certainly noting my movements with my hands, with a perpetual cigarette, etc. Some of my movements – people who know me have said, oh yes, he's got that. But I'm sure he wasn't imitating. He just registered it.

As I said, I did find him very shy. When he was in maximum make-up, with all the sores and lesions on his face, he wouldn't eat with the rest of the cast and crew in the hospital dining room. It was as though he actually had the disease and didn't like being seen like that.

MG: He does have a tendency to live the role while he's doing it. One might say that's more typical of American actors.

POTTER: He doesn't ask questions like those American actors ask – about the character's father, or childhood. It's as though he has asked the questions of himself. Gambon would never talk around the part. You wouldn't feel those gears being shifted, and yet that sort of occupation of the part must be going on in him.

MG: What questions would he ask you about the role?

POTTER: Hardly any. What sort of accent? The discussion came up at the read-through when he dropped into a pseudo-American. I said I didn't think that was appropriate, and he immediately dropped it.

You wouldn't be surprised to encounter him in a Dickens novel, as a kind of accountant's clerk or solicitor's clerk wearing patent leather shoes, who sits on a high stool like the other clerks – and does amazing things when he locks the office door. There's something of that in him which comes out in his acting.

Peter Hall, 4 July 1990

We did *Betrayal* and I watched with fascination the growth of this extraordinary talent. Ralph Richardson and I were both Gambon-watchers. Richardson used to say to me, 'This is the coming leading actor, because he is such a chameleon.' He coined the phrase 'The Great Gambon'. We had all seen him in *The Norman Conquests*, in which he demonstrated that extraordinary comic ability. But the weight, the heroic quality and the compassion and what Ralph Richardson recognised – he had it himself. Both endorse the faults and lunacies of a character, the unsympathetic side, and by doing that make the man more understandable and, finally, sympathetic. Both have the capacity to play any class of person. It's quite rare in an actor to be able to be convincingly a plumber and a Shake-spearean king. And Ralph and Gambon can both do that.

I wanted to do *Galileo* at the National. I just thought of the potency and size of Gambon. He's a gentle actor with the most catastrophic power that he can unleash. That is to me the danger of him onstage. I thought it would be wonderful for Galileo. Five leading directors turned him and me down, and I wouldn't let them do it without Gambon. I persuaded John Dexter to do it.

Gambon seems to be able to turn his sense of physical bulk on and off at will. He can play small men of small temperament and he can play vast brutes. I shall always remember the physical sense he brought to *A View from the Bridge*. You felt that the man worked with his hands and his muscles. It was a huge frame.

Michael has become a great actor, or been recognised as a great actor, somewhat late in life. He's passed the age of a romantic juvenile, but I certainly think he's a leading man. He could play somebody in love, somebody with passion. I think he can play pretty near anything. To me, he is like those great actors of France and Germany who are marinated in every kind of classical role, and seem able to do anything. I think he gets inside a character and changes himself much more than the conventional classical actor. He has the ability to be a winner or a loser, to be sexy or unsexy. He can switch off different areas of his personality and remake himself. I think that's called genius. How does he do it? I don't suppose he can tell you. Most actors bring the part to themselves. In some curious way, Michael takes himself to the part. Fate gave him genius, but he uses it as a craftsman.

Simon Russell Beale, 15 November 2002

Because Mosca [Russell Beale's role in *Volpone*] does all the work, I think Michael [as Volpone] saw himself as coming on and doing the odd big number, the seduction of Celia, or the mountebank scene. I think it was cleverer than I realised at the time because I was quite puritan about how you do plays.

The relationship between the two [Volpone and Mosca] is very, very funny. I loved working with him, and I think he loved working with me. And we're completely different, not in theatrical backgrounds, but in attitude.

I think he takes acting deeply seriously. But I think he had an idea of joy onstage that was above and beyond the text. He knew the play could survive if those two central characters were having as much fun as Michael and Simon were – which I hadn't realised. That was the difference between us, but, as I say, there are more similarities than differences in the sense that he's 'RSC', as I was.

Deborah Warner, 10 May 2003

I think he is one of the greatest actors there ever ever was. He's heavenly, super great. And he's the most terrible prankster. He is absolutely the essence of the thing but he gets bored very quickly – isn't that the point? In film I learned quite quickly that you have to film Michael's first rehearsal. I think he's the real acting creature. He's definitive and terribly terribly funny and very, very dangerous. But, in life, dangerous. His stories come out in many different forms. I'm not sure there is much line between reality and imagination, which is why he's marvellous.

In *Last September* I gave him one of the first electricity generators to play with in his role in the film. He was terribly happy. That's what he needs. He's a precision engineer. He has an amazing gun collection and his passion is 18th-century. He needs to be entertained. All those big brain actors do – Maggie [Smith] or Fiona [Shaw] or him. They absolutely need to be fed. They're tigers. I'd adore to work with him again. I love him. But he entertains me. He and Maggie have marvellous reputations of being tricky and they are not at all. They just have to be fed.

218

Acknowledgements

I want to thank Nick Hern, who created this series and remains the quintessential British publisher of books about theatre; those mentioned above who spoke to me about Gambon (Alan Ayckbourn, Harold Pinter, Adrian Noble, Dennis Potter, Peter Hall, Simon Russell Beale, Deborah Warner, Nicholas Hytner and Douglas Hodge). Others who have talked to me about him over the years include Laurence Olivier, Peggy Ramsay, Arthur Miller, Fiona Shaw, Larry Dalzell, Stephen Moore, Oliver Cotton and Michael Frayn. As always, my gratitude goes to Ann and Ethan Gussow for sharing nights at the theatre (many with Gambon onstage) – and Ann for her invaluable advice and suggestions in editing. Carol Coburn in New York and Pamela Kent in London, both of the *New York Times*, have been helpful in keeping me up to date with theatrical events in their cities. The root of this book was my profile about Gambon that appeared in the January 28, 1991 issue of the *New Yorker*. Robert Gottlieb, as the editor of that magazine at that time, accepted the idea and the profile when it was finished and Patrick Crow edited it and my other *New Yorker* profiles (which were written for William Shawn, to whom I am permanently indebted). Some of the material in the Introduction appeared in different form in the *New Yorker*. The last four conversations were conducted specifically for this book.

Books consulted include: *Olivier at Work*, compiled by the Royal National Theatre; *A Sense of Direction: Life at the Royal Court* by William Gaskill; *Theatre at Work: The Story of the National Theatre's Production of Brecht's Galileo* by Jim Hiley; *The Story of Unity Theatre* by Colin Chambers; *Fight & Kick & Bite: The Life and Work of Dennis Potter* by W. Stephen Gilbert; *Dennis Potter: Seeing the Blossom, Two Interviews and a Lecture*; *Straight Face* by Nigel Hawthorne; *Alan Ayckbourn: Grinning at the Edge* by Paul Allen; *The Crafty Art of Playmaking* by Alan Ayckbourn, and *Beside Myself: An Autobiography* by Antony Sher.

Most of all, of course, I want to thank Michael Gambon for his openness in welcoming me into his world, for his expansive humour, his good company – and his brilliance as an actor.

Principal Roles

Theatre

1962   Second Gentleman in *Othello*, the Gaiety Theatre in Dublin: Gambon's first professional appearance onstage.

1963-67   Small roles in *Hamlet, Saint Joan, The Recruiting Officer, Andorra, Philoctetes, Othello, The Royal Hunt of the Sun, The Crucible, Mother Courage, Love for Love, Juno and the Paycock* and *The Storm*, National Theatre at the Old Vic.

1967-68   *Events While Guarding the Bofors Gun, A Severed Head, Peer Gynt* and the title role in *Othello* among other parts, Birmingham Repertory company,

1968   *Macbeth*, the Forum in Billingham.

1969   *In Celebration* and *Coriolanus*, Liverpool Playhouse.

1970-71   *The Plebeians Rehearse the Uprising, Major Barbara, Henry VIII,* Royal Shakespeare Company.

1973   *Not Drowning But Waving* at the Yvonne Arnaud Theatre, Guildford.

1975   *The Norman Conquests*, the Globe Theatre, London; *The Zoo Story*, Open Air Theatre, London.

1976   Replaced Alan Bates in *Otherwise Engaged*, Queens Theatre.

1977   *Just Between Ourselves*, Queens Theatre.

1978   *Alice's Boys*, Savoy Theatre; *Betrayal, Close of Play*, National Theatre.

1979-80   *Sisterly Feelings*, National Theatre.

1980   *Galileo, Tales from Hollywood*, National Theatre.

1982-83   *King Lear, Antony and Cleopatra*, Royal Shakespeare Company, Stratford-upon-Avon; later transferred to the Barbican.

1985   *Old Times*, Theatre Royal, Haymarket; *A Chorus of Disapproval*, National Theatre.

1987   *A View from the Bridge, A Small Family Business, Tons of Money*, National Theatre.

1988   *Mountain Language*, National Theatre; *Uncle Vanya*, Vaudeville Theatre.

1989   *Veterans' Day*, Theatre Royal, Haymarket

1990   *Man of the Moment*, Globe Theatre; *Othello, Taking Steps*, Stephen Joseph Theatre, Scarborough.

1995	*Volpone, Skylight*, National Theatre.
1996	*Skylight*, Broadway.
1997	*Tom and Clem*, Aldwych Theatre.
1998	*The Unexpected Man*, Royal Shakespeare Company.
2000	*Cressida*, Almeida Theatre at the Albery.
2001	*The Caretaker*, Comedy Theatre.
2002	*A Number*, Royal Court Theatre.
2004	*Endgame*, Albery Theatre.

Film

1985	*Turtle Diary.*
1989	*The Cook, the Thief, His Wife and Her Lover; A Dry White Season.*
1992	*Toys.*
1994	*A Man of No Importance; The Browning Version.*
1996	*Mary Reilly.*
1997	*The Wings of the Dove; The Gambler.*
1998	*Dancing at Lughnasa.*
1999	*Plunkett and Macleane; Sleepy Hollow; Last September; The Insider.*
2001	*Gosford Park; Charlotte Gray.*
2002	*Ali G Indahouse.*
2003	*The Actors; Open Range; Sylvia.*
2004	*Being Julia; Layer Cake; Harry Potter and the Prisoner of Azkaban.*

Television and Radio

1968	*The Borderers.*
1972	*The Challengers.*
1986	*The Singing Detective.*
1990	*The Heat of the Day; Betrayal*, BBC Radio Three.
1993-94	*Inspector Maigret.*
1999	*Wives and Daughters.*
2000	*Longitude, Endgame.*
2001	*Perfect Strangers*; in US (2002) as *Almost Strangers.*
2002	*Path to War.*
2003	*The Lost Prince; Angels in America.*

Index of Titles and Authors